Cooking with Your
INSTANT POT® MINI

Cooking with Your
INSTANT POT® MINI

100 QUICK & EASY RECIPES
FOR 3-QUART MODELS

Heather Schlueter

STERLING EPICURE
New York

STERLING EPICURE
New York

An Imprint of Sterling Publishing Co., Inc.
1166 Avenue of the Americas
New York, NY 10036

ISBN 978-1-45493192-8

Distributed in Canada by Sterling Publishing Co., Inc.
c/o Canadian Manda Group, 664 Annette Street
Toronto, Ontario M6S 2C8, Canada
Distributed in the United Kingdom by GMC Distribution Services
Castle Place, 166 High Street, Lewes, East Sussex BN7 1XU, England
Distributed in Australia by NewSouth Books
45 Beach Street, Coogee, NSW 2034, Australia

For information about custom editions,
special sales, and premium and corporate purchases,
please contact Sterling Special Sales at
800-805-5489 or specialsales@sterlingpublishing.com.

Manufactured in Canada

2 4 6 8 10 9 7 5 3 1

sterlingpublishing.com

Interior design by Gavin Motnyk
Cover design by Jo Obarowski
Photography by Bill Milne, except: Color insert (spaghetti and meatballs) ©Joshua Resnick/Shutterstock;
Back cover (upper left and lower right) ©mphilips007/iStock, (upper right) ©dr911/iStock.

CONTENTS

COOKING WITH YOUR INSTANT POT® MINI . . . . *vii*

MY TIPS FOR SUCCESS . . . . *ix*

EGGS & BREAKFAST *1*

RICE, GRAINS & PASTA *25*

BEANS *39*

MEAT & POULTRY *51*

SOUPS, STEWS & CHILI *85*

VEGGIES *113*

DESSERTS *133*

ABOUT THE AUTHOR *153*

ACKNOWLEDGMENTS *154*

INDEX *155*

COOKING WITH YOUR INSTANT POT® MINI

It's been called the "miracle pot," the "genius pot," and the "it-made-me-love-cooking-again-pot." (And, of course, the ever-popular "Instapot.") There's no doubt about it: the Instant Pot® has changed the way we cook today. Cooking with the Instant Pot is quick, easy, and fun, and home cooks, including me, enjoy the versatility and ease of getting delicious, creative meals on the table in a hurry. Plus, every meal can be a one-pot dish making cleanup a breeze.

The folks at Instant Pot—geniuses that they are—produced the Instant Pot Mini, the 3-quart version of the very popular 6- and 8-quart models, and pot heads like me are obsessed.

As expected, the compact models are hugely popular. It is perfect for home cooks looking for smaller portions or as a second (or third?) device for those who want to own multiple pots for culinary creation.

Although there is a plethora of recipes for the Instant Pot community, not all available recipes can just be "downsized" for the Instant Pot Mini. It's a pressure cooker after all, and the food-to-liquid-to-spices ratio is critical for tasty success. That is why I wrote this book. All 100 recipes you'll find here are specifically created for the Instant Pot Mini models.

With this book you'll be able to enjoy wonderful recipes without complicated conversions. After all, who wants to figure out what is one half of one third of a teaspoon, right? Will these recipes really work in your Instant Pot Mini? The answer is yes! The velvety Creamy Mac & Cheese (page 36), the tasty Sweet & Spicy Asian Ribs (page 74), the classic Mississippi Pot Roast (page 64), and of course, the well-loved Mini New York Cheesecakes with Fresh Fruit (page 134) will all work—no calculations necessary. Just follow the simple instructions and prepare to be amazed by your extraordinary creations.

—HEATHER SCHLUETER

PC MAX —— 2/3

—— 1/2

MY TIPS FOR SUCCESS

Understanding cooking with your Instant Pot appliance involves a learning curve for all. But jump right on it and I think you will become an expert in no time! These are some of my tips and tricks for delicious results using the Instant Pot Mini.

It Takes Some Time to Come to Pressure

Yes, Instant Pot multicookers cook meals far faster than traditional cooking methods. But it is important to keep in mind that the appliance takes time to build pressure. Many existing recipes are a bit misleading in that they only discuss the cooking time. Depending on the temperature and volume of food placed in the inner pot, the pressurization time can be anywhere from a couple of minutes to more than 15 minutes. The cooking time begins after the Instant Pot display reads "on" as it comes to full pressure. Next, the pressure-keeping time will appear once the appliance has reached full pressure. To help you plan accordingly, I have provided "hands-on time" (food prep time), "cooking time" (the amount of time to set the LED Display to cook), and "total time," which includes pressurization and release times.

Use the Utensils That Come with the Unit

Yes, the plastic utensils that are packaged with the Instant Pot multicooker are easy to overlook, toss in the back of a drawer and never use. But I think they are actually helpful. The curve of the spatula and the handle fit inside the appliance like pieces of a puzzle. And the measuring cup holds the exact amount of liquid needed when using the steaming rack.

Consider Buying Additional Silicone Rings

Silicone is wonderful. It creates a perfect airtight seal necessary for proper pressure cooking in the appliance. That being said, it does have a tendency to absorb odors from previously cooked foods. Many users, including me, prefer to purchase additional silicone sealing rings and switch them out when making savory or sweet dishes. Additional silicone rings can be found on the Internet, but I recommend that you use only Genuine Instant Pot silicone rings, as using any other rings will void your warranty. (Check your appliance manual about this.) When purchasing silicone rings, be sure to choose the right size for your lid.

The Pot Has a Lid Holder

Easily disguised, the slots on the side handles of the appliance double as a resting place for the lid. When the lid is off, the two plastic extensions at the base of the handle fit perfectly into those slots, securely holding the lid at a 90-degree angle. Genius!

Altitude Does Make a Difference

Those at high altitude may have to increase the cooking times by a few minutes. Increase cooking time by 15 percent at 5,000 feet and an additional 5 percent for every additional 1,000 feet.

Protect Your Cabinets from Pressure

The applinace releases steam from the pressure valve on the lid at the end of the cooking cycle. Although the valve is on the back of the lid, be aware of low-hanging overhead cabinets. Over time, repeated steam exposure can discolor the underside or faces of the cabinets. To avoid this issue, take precaution by rotating the unit and pulling it to the edge of the counter so the release valve is not directly under the overhanging cabinets.

What's with All Those Buttons?

At first glance an Instant Pot multicooker can be a little intimidating. But it doesn't take long to realize that the genius is in its simplicity. All of the buttons are presets and designed to make cooking simple. Though preset settings have determined times, cooking modes, and pressure levels, the settings can be changed manually by pressing the buttons repeatedly until the desired setting is achieved. Here is a brief description of each function button, which can also be found in the Instant Pot manual.

DISPLAY PANEL This panel indicates time, mode, and pressure level. The "Less," "Normal," and "More" indicator represents the temperature. The "Low" and "High" indicator represents cooking

mode. The vast majority of pressure cooking will be done at normal mode and high pressure.

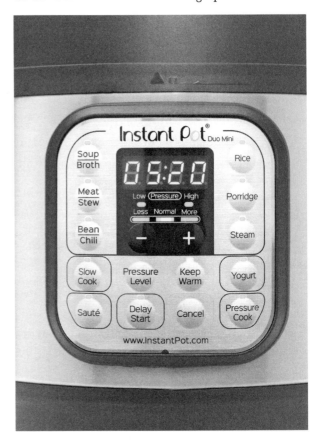

SOUP/BROTH Defaults to 30 minutes at normal cooking mode and high pressure. Press the button again to change to low pressure for clear broth soups.

MEAT/STEW Defaults to 35 minutes at normal cooking mode and high pressure.

BEAN/CHILI Defaults to 30 minutes at normal cooking mode and high pressure.

EGG (DUO PLUS) Defaults to 5 minutes at high pressure.

SLOW COOK Defaults to 4 hours at normal cooking mode.

SAUTÉ Defaults to 30 minutes at normal cooking mode.

RICE This is a fully automated program for white rice only and cannot be altered. It senses the amount of rice and will adjust the time automatically. It is set to low pressure.

PORRIDGE Defaults to 20 minutes at normal cooking mode and high pressure.

STEAM Defaults to 10 minutes at normal cooking mode and high pressure.

STERILIZE (DUO PLUS) Defaults to 30 minutes at normal cooking mode and low pressure. Used to sterilize canning equipment and baby bottles, among other things.

YOGURT Defaults to boil at high cooking mode for 8 hours.

PRESSURE COOK Defaults to 35 minutes at normal cooking mode and high pressure. This is the most used button, and you will likely change the time for this one frequently.

PRESSURE LEVEL Press this to toggle the pressure level between low and high.

DELAY START This can be set to delay the start of any cooking function.

KEEP WARM This will automatically engage at the end of a cooking cycle and can be turned off manually by pressing the cancel button.

CANCEL This is the "Off" button. Press this to turn the unit off or to turn off one function before switching to another function.

"+" AND "-" These are used to adjust the cooking time after a cooking function has been selected.

LEARN THE THREE TYPES OF PRESSURE RELEASE

The recipes in this book call for different types of pressure releases. Learn the difference to achieve the best results.

QUICK RELEASE As soon as the pressure-keeping time reaches zero, turn the steam release handle to the Venting position to let steam out until the float valve drops down and you no longer hear steam coming out. Never pull out the steam release handle while releasing steam, as escaping steam is extremely hot and can scald. Additionally, avoid putting your hands directly over the release valve.

NATURAL RELEASE After the pressure-keeping time reaches zero, allow the cooker to cool naturally until the float valve drops down. Depending on the type and quantity of food inside the inner pot, a full natural release can take anywhere from about 10 minutes to up to an hour. Many recipes call for a natural release for a period of time (for example, "natural release for 15 minutes"). This allows some of the pressure to naturally release.

After that time occurs, you then turn the valve to the Venting position to release the remaining pressure.

SLOW RELEASE Recipes that contain a lot of starch such as pastas or beans often suggest a slow release. When a recipe has starchy foods, the steam within the appliance will collect a fair amount of starch. That starch may come through the valve during a quick release, which can cause spitting and create a bit of a mess. A slow release is when you turn the pressure valve toward the Venting position but not all the way at once. Turn the valve just a little bit and hold it stationary as the pressure releases and until the valve stops spitting. Using a long-handled spoon or spatula ensures that your hands stay clear of the steam release valve. As the pressure releases, turn the valve a little bit more toward the Venting position. Continue this method until all pressure has fully released.

My Cooking Suggestions

Here are a few basic ideas to keep in mind as you prepare meals with your appliance.

Cornstarch Is Your Friend

One difference with pressure cooking that takes a bit of an adjustment is the amount of liquid in the inner pot after the dish is cooked. If, at the end of the cooking cycle, you would like a thicker sauce, simply mix a couple of tablespoons of cornstarch (or potato flakes) with a couple of tablespoons of water to make a slurry. Once the dish is fully cooked, turn on the sauté function, let the liquid come to a boil, and add the slurry, stirring until the desired thickness is reached.

Crisp Things Up in an Oven or on the Grill

The Instant Pot multicooker cooks with pressure and steam. It's what makes meat fall-off-the-bone tender, and it's why dishes can be cooked so quickly. What it doesn't do is leave food crunchy or crispy. So if you're looking for golden-brown crispy chicken skin, or a nice char on your ribs, make sure to toss the meat into a hot oven or onto a grill for a few minutes after the pressure-cooking process.

Do Not Overfill the Inner Pot

There is a "⅔" marker on the inside of the Instant Pot inner pot. Use it as a guide so you don't overfill the inner pot. If you fill ingredients past this line, there will not be enough space within the inner pot for pressure to build and seal properly. I have found there are a few exceptions to this—if stacking smaller dishes within the pot, such as ramekins and mini springform pans, the height of those stacked can exceed the ⅔ line because there will be enough space around them to still enable proper pressure and sealing. Also, if you are cooking starchy ingredients that will foam, such as rice or beans, make sure to not exceed the "½" line.

Ensure the Bottom Is Clean

Many recipes call for ingredients to be sautéed before pressure cooking, and with the Instant Pot multicooker, there is no need to dirty another pan. However, this highly praised feature does leave brown bits on the bottom of the inner pot. It is critical to make sure to deglaze the inner pot and scrape the bottom clean (a wooden spoon or spatula works best for this) before switching to the pressure cook function. If the bottom of the inner pot is coated with brown bits or a thick paste, the appliance will not seal properly.

Pot-in-Pot Cooking Method

The versatility of the Instant Pot multicooker is one of the reasons it is enormously popular. Many dishes that are traditionally baked in an oven can be cooked much faster in the appliance with the "Pot-In-Pot" method. Dishes such as casseroles and many desserts can be placed in a baking dish (such as a ramekin) or pan (such as a springform pan) that are smaller than the inner pot of the appliance. The smaller dish is placed on the steam rack inside the Instant Pot inner pot, which allows the dish to be cooked but not directly submerged in the liquid required to bring the appliance to pressure.

If the smaller dish within the inner pot is a tight squeeze, simply use aluminum foil to create a "sling" that will allow you to lower and raise the dish without needing additional room for your fingers. Take a piece of aluminum foil approximately 20 inches (50 centimeters) long and fold it over lengthwise several times until it forms a 3-inch-wide (8 cm) narrow strip of foil that is 20 inches (50 cm) long. Place this strip under the bottom and up the sides of the dish you are placing on top of the steam rack inside the Instant Pot inner pot. Use the ends of the steam rack of foil as "handles" with which you can lower and raise the dish. Just make sure to tuck the ends fully inside the appliance when putting on the lid so it does not interfere with the normal sealing process.

Just Because You Can Cook It in the Appliance Doesn't Mean You Should

This miracle appliance makes one start to believe everything can be cooked in it. But, the real question is: should it be? There are types of food that are better cooked in their traditional manner—a flavorful ribeye steak is still best cooked in a cast iron pan or on a very hot grill; delicate beef tenderloin should still be done in an oven. And crispy egg rolls? Yes, they still need frying. Although it is very tempting to throw anything and everything into the appliance, stick to what works best, and you and your family will love the results!

EGGS & BREAKFAST

EASY-PEEL HARD-BOILED EGGS 2

SOFT-BOILED EGGS 3

PERFECTLY POACHED EGGS 4

CRUSTLESS QUICHE 5

MOIST CHOCOLATE CHIP BANANA NUT BREAD 6

CLASSIC FRENCH TOAST CASSEROLE 8

BLUEBERRY-ALMOND FRENCH TOAST CASSEROLE 10

STEAMED BOSTON BROWN BREAD 12

RASPBERRY COFFEE CAKE 14

BLUEBERRY-ALMOND CRUNCH COFFEE CAKE 16

COCONUT-BANANA STEEL CUT OATMEAL 18

BLUEBERRY-CREAM STEEL CUT OATMEAL 19

GIANT OATMEAL PANCAKE 20

VANILLA YOGURT 22

Easy-Peel Hard-Boiled Eggs

Yield: 6 Eggs | Hands-on Time: 1 Minute | Cooking Time: 7 Minutes | Total Time: 10 Minutes |
Buttons to Use: Pressure Cook | Release Type: Quick Release

Hard-boiled eggs (they're not actually "boiled" in the Instant Pot) are often a go-to first-time recipe, and for good reason—the eggs are nothing short of a miracle. Perfect every time, and they practically peel themselves!

6 eggs

salt and pepper to taste

1. Place the steam rack into the Instant Pot inner pot. Add ¾ cup (180 ml) water.

2. Place the eggs on top of the steam rack (a collapsible steamer basket also works well), ensuring the eggs are not touching the water below the steam rack.

3. Secure the lid and turn the valve to the Sealing position.

4. Press the Pressure Cook button and set the time to 7 minutes.

5. Once cooking is complete, turn the valve to the Venting position to release the pressure. When all the pressure is released, carefully remove the lid. Immediately remove the eggs and place them in a bowl with cool water until they can be handled easily.

6. Peel and serve with salt and pepper. If not serving immediately, eggs will keep in the refrigerator for up to 1 week.

Soft-Boiled Eggs

Yield: 6 Eggs | Hands-on Time: 1 Minute | Cooking Time: 1 Minute | Total Time: 5 Minutes |
Buttons to Use: Pressure Cook | Release Type: Quick Release

Soft-boiled eggs served over toast or an English muffin makes for a great start to the day. But make sure to pay attention to the time if you're looking for soft-boiled perfection. Remove immediately and you'll be amazed with the results.

6 eggs

salt and pepper to taste

toast for serving

1. Place the steam rack into the Instant Pot inner pot. Add ¾ cup (180 ml) water.

2. Place the eggs on top of the steam rack. (The Genuine Instant Pot Silicone Steamer Basket also works well.) Ensure that the eggs are not touching the water below the steam rack.

3. Secure the lid and turn the valve to the Sealing position.

4. Select the Pressure Cook button and set the time to 1 minute.

5. Once cooking is complete, turn the valve to the Venting position to release the pressure. When all the pressure is released, carefully remove the lid. Immediately remove the eggs and place them in a bowl with cool water until they can easily be handled.

6. Peel and serve over toast with salt and pepper. If not serving immediately, eggs will keep in the refrigerator for up to two days.

Perfectly Poached Eggs

Yield: 2 Eggs | Hands-on Time: 1 Minute | Cooking Time: 0 Minutes | Total Time: 5 Minutes |
Buttons to Use: Pressure Cook; LOW PRESSURE | Release Type: Quick Release

It's not a typo—you can have warm, comforting, and runny-in-the-middle poached eggs with zero cooking time. The time it takes to pressure up and release is all that's needed. For this recipe, you will need two small ramekins, 5 ounces (150 ml) each.

cooking spray

2 eggs

TIP: To change the pressure level to low, push the Pressure Cook button and then push the Pressure Level button. The indicator on the display toggles back and forth between high and low pressure. Do not forget to check the pressure level the next time you use the Instant Pot.

1. Spray the ramekins with cooking spray and put 1 teaspoon of water in each. Crack one egg into each ramekin.

2. Place the steam rack in the Instant Pot inner pot and add ¾ cup (180 ml) water. Position the ramekins side by side on top of the steam rack.

3. Secure the lid and turn the valve to the Sealing position. Press the Pressure Cook button. Then press the Pressure Level button to set to Low pressure. Set the time to 0 minutes.

4. After full pressure is reached, the pressure-keeping time will begin. As soon as you hear the beep indicating the time has "started," turn the valve to the Venting position to release the pressure. When all pressure is released, carefully remove the lid, remove the ramekins, and enjoy.

Crustless Quiche

Yield: 4 Servings | Hands-on Time: 5 Minutes | Cooking Time: 20 Minutes | Total Time: 30 Minutes | Buttons to Use: Pressure Cook | Release Type: Quick Release

Quiche doesn't need to be saved for special occasions. This egg, ham, Cheddar, and green onion dish comes together in 5 minutes and is on the table in 30 minutes. Plus, it's great with leftover ham! This recipe requires two mini springform pans, 4 inches (100 mm) in diameter and 15-ounce (450 ml) capacity, that can be stacked on top of each other during the cooking process.

---

5 eggs

1½ cups (175 g) shredded Cheddar cheese

1 cup (150 g) diced cooked ham

2 green onions, white and light-green parts sliced

½ teaspoon dried thyme

¼ teaspoon pepper

cooking spray

1. In a large bowl, lightly beat the eggs. Add all the remaining ingredients and blend well.

2. Spray two mini 15-ounce (450 ml) springform pans with the cooking spray. Add the egg mixture, dividing equally between the two pans.

3. Place the steam rack in the Instant Pot inner pot. Add ¾ cup (180 ml) water. Carefully place one springform pan on top of the steam rack. Stack the other pan on top of the first. Pull both springform pans toward the front of the Instant Pot so they don't interfere with the venting mechanism that is toward the back of the pot. Secure the lid, ensuring the valve is turned to the Sealing position. Press the Pressure Cook button and set the time to 20 minutes.

4. Once cooking is complete, turn the valve to the Venting position to release all the pressure. When the pressure is released, carefully remove the lid and remove the springform pans using oven mitts. Let quiches sit in pans for 5 minutes. Then run a knife along the inside of the pans to release the quiches from the sides. Remove the side of each pan and run a knife under the bottom of the quiche to release it from the bottom. Transfer to a plate and serve immediately.

Moist Chocolate Chip Banana Nut Bread

Yield: 4 Servings | Hands-on Time: 5 Minutes | Cooking Time: 45 Minutes | Total Time: 60 Minutes | Buttons to Use: Pressure Cook | Release Type: Quick Release

Moist, dense, and full of flavor, this banana nut bread is great for breakfast, a snack, or even dessert. Add a pat of butter when it's hot out of the pot. You need two mini springform pans—4-inch (10 cm) diameter and 15-ounce (450 ml) capacity—for this dish.

2 ripe bananas, peeled

4 tablespoons butter, melted and cooled

1 egg

1 cup (120 g) flour

¼ cup (50 g) sugar

1 teaspoon baking powder

¼ cup (45 g) high-quality semi-sweet chocolate chips

¼ cup (30 g) walnut pieces

1 teaspoon vanilla

¼ teaspoon cinnamon

additional butter for serving, if desired

1. In a medium bowl, smash bananas with a fork until lumps are gone. Stir in the butter and egg.

2. In a small bowl whisk together flour, sugar, and baking powder.

3. Add the flour mixture to the bananas and then stir in the chocolate chips, walnut pieces, vanilla, and cinnamon. Mix well.

4. Pour the batter into two mini springform pans that have been sprayed with cooking spray, divided equally.

5. Place the steam rack into the Instant Pot inner pot and add ¾ cup (180 ml) water.

6. Carefully place one springform pan on top of the steam rack. Stack the other pan on top of the first. Pull pans toward the front of the inner pot so they do not interfere with the venting mechanism.

7. Secure the lid, ensuring the valve is turned to the Sealing position.

8. Press the Pressure Cook button and set the time to 45 minutes.

9. Once cooking is complete, turn the valve to the Venting position to release the pressure. When all the pressure is released, carefully remove the lid.

10. Remove the springform pans and set on a cooling rack. After 10 minutes, remove the springform rims of pans. Serve warm with a pat of butter, if desired.

Classic French Toast Casserole

Yield: 4 Servings | Hands-on Time: 5 Minutes | Cooking Time: 25 Minutes | Total Time : 40 Minutes |
Buttons to Use: Pressure Cook | Release Type: Quick Release

With hints of cinnamon, vanilla, and brown sugar, you'll feel like you're sitting down to a holiday breakfast the moment you taste this warm, gooey, chunky French toast casserole. This recipe is made using the "Pot-in-Pot" method. You will need the steam rack and an ovenproof baking dish for this method. This recipe uses a 1-quart (1 L) round baking casserole dish with a 5½-inch (14 cm) diameter.

---

1 cup (240 ml) whole milk

2 eggs

¼ cup (50 g) brown sugar

1 teaspoon vanilla

½ teaspoon cinnamon

4 thick slices of French bread cut into 2-inch (5 cm) pieces

cooking spray

maple syrup for serving, if desired

TIP: Please see the description of "Pot-in-Pot Cooking Method" in "Cooking Tips" section of this book on page xiv.

1. In a large bowl whisk together the milk, eggs, brown sugar, vanilla, and cinnamon until well blended. Fold in the bread pieces until they are well coated.

2. Spray the baking dish with cooking spray and pour the bread mixture into the dish.

3. Place the steam rack into the Instant Pot inner pot and add ¾ cup (180 ml) water. Carefully lower the baking dish into the inner pot and place on the steam rack.

4. Secure the lid, ensuring the valve is turned to the Sealing position.

5. Press the Pressure Cook button and set the time to 25 minutes.

6. Once cooking is complete, turn the valve to the Venting position. When all the pressure has released, remove the lid and carefully lift out the baking dish using oven mitts. Let the casserole sit for 5 minutes and then serve hot with warm maple syrup, if desired.

Blueberry-Almond French Toast Casserole

Yield: 4 Servings | Hands-on Time: 5 Minutes | Cooking Time: 25 Minutes | Total Time: 40 Minutes |
Buttons to Use: Pressure Cook | Release Type: Quick Release

Tangy blueberries and crunchy almonds take this French toast to a whole new level, yet it's simple enough to become an everyday favorite. This recipe uses a 1-quart (1 L) round baking casserole dish that has a 5½-inch (14 cm) diameter. (Note: see "Pot-in-Pot Cooking Method" in the tips section on page xiv.)

1 cup (240 ml) whole milk

2 eggs

¼ cup (50 g) brown sugar

½ teaspoon almond extract

½ teaspoon cinnamon

1 cup (150 g) fresh blueberries, or ½ cup (75 g) frozen, thawed

4 thick slices French bread cut into 2-inch (5 cm) pieces

cooking spray

powdered sugar, slivered almonds, and additional blueberries for serving

maple syrup for serving, if desired

1. In a large bowl whisk together the milk, eggs, brown sugar, almond extract, and cinnamon until well blended. Fold in the blueberries and bread pieces until well coated.

2. Spray the baking dish with cooking spray and pour the bread mixture into the dish.

3. Place the steam rack into the Instant Pot inner pot and add ¾ cup (180 ml) water. Carefully lower the baking dish onto the steam rack.

4. Secure the lid, ensuring the valve is turned to the Sealing position.

5. Press the Pressure Cook button and set the time to 25 minutes.

6. Once cooking is complete, turn the valve to the Venting position. When all the pressure has released, remove the lid and carefully lift out the baking dish using oven mitts. Let it sit 5 minutes before serving it hot, topped with a dusting of powdered sugar, slivered almonds, and additional blueberries. Serve with maple syrup, if desired.

Steamed Boston Brown Bread

Yield: 8 Slices from 2 Jars | Hands-on Time: 10 Minutes | Cooking Time: 45 Minutes | Total Time: 75 Minutes | Buttons to Use: Pressure Cook | Release Type: Quick Release

This old-fashioned, dense and rich bread is loaded with plump raisins and is delicious when topped with a schmear of cream cheese. This recipe fills two 16-ounce (480 ml) canning jars; however, only one will fit into the Instant Pot Mini at a time. You will need to cook this recipe in two batches or halve the recipe to make only one loaf. You will need two 16-ounce (480 ml) wide-mouth ovenproof canning jars, aluminum foil, and kitchen twine.

½ cup (60 g) all-purpose white flour

½ cup (60 g) rye flour

½ cup (70 g) cornmeal

1 teaspoon baking powder

½ teaspoon salt

½ cup (160 ml) dark molasses

1 cup (240 ml) whole milk

1 teaspoon vanilla

½ cup (75 g) raisins

cooking spray

butter and/or cream cheese for serving, if desired

1. In a medium bowl, mix together the white flour, rye flour, cornmeal, baking powder, and salt. In a separate small bowl, mix together the molasses, milk, and vanilla.

2. Add the molasses mixture to the dry flour mixture and blend well. Fold in the raisins.

3. Spray the inside of the jars with cooking spray.

4. Pour the batter into the two prepared jars, divided equally. Each jar should be approximately two-thirds full. Cover the jars with aluminum foil, securing the foil around the jars with kitchen twine.

5. Place the steam rack into the Instant Pot inner pot. Place one jar on the steam rack. Fill the Instant Pot inner pot with water until it reaches one-third of the way up the side of the jar.

6. Secure the lid, ensuring the valve is turned to the Sealing position.

7. Press Pressure Cook and set the time to 45 minutes.

8. Once cooking is complete, turn the valve to the Venting position to release the pressure. When all the pressure is released, remove the lid. Carefully remove the jar using oven mitts.

9. Repeat steps 6 through 8 with the remaining batter-filled jar.

10. Remove the foil from the jars. Slide a knife down and around the inside of the jar to release the bread. Carefully turn the jar over and shake until the bread comes out. Let cool a few minutes, then slice crosswise. Each jar should yield 4 to 6 slices. Top each slice with butter or cream cheese, and serve immediately.

Raspberry Coffee Cake

Yield: 4 Servings | Hands-on Time: 10 Minutes | Cooking Time: 30 Minutes | Total Time: 45 Minutes |
Buttons to Use: Pressure Cook | Release Type: Quick Release

Sink your teeth into this tasty, sweet cake bursting with pockets of fresh raspberry flavor. This recipe requires two 15-ounce (450 ml) mini springform pans, 4 inches (10 cm) in diameter. Cook them one at a time for best results. It is possible to stack them and cook at the same time, but the bottom cake will not rise as well.

FOR CAKE

4 ounces (115 g) cream cheese, room temperature

¼ cup (50 g) sugar

1 egg white

1 cup (125 g) fresh raspberries

¾ cup (90 g) flour

1 teaspoon baking powder

½ cup (120 g) sour cream

3 tablespoons butter, melted

1 egg plus 1 egg yolk

½ teaspoon vanilla

baking spray

FOR TOPPING

½ cup (100 g) brown sugar

¼ cup (30 g) flour

2 tablespoons chilled butter, cut into small chunks

1. In a medium bowl, mix the cream cheese, sugar, and egg white. Using a hand blender, blend until the mixture is smooth. Fold in fresh raspberries and set aside.

2. In a separate medium bowl, whisk together the flour and baking powder. Add sour cream, melted butter, egg and egg yolk, and vanilla to the dry mixture. Mix well using a spatula. Add the cream cheese mixture and mix until combined.

3. Spray two 15-ounce (450 ml) mini springform pans with baking spray. Pour the batter evenly into the springform pans until three-quarters full.

4. To make the topping, combine brown sugar and flour in a small bowl. Cut in the chilled butter chunks with two forks until the mixture is crumbly. Top each cake, dividing the topping mixture between the springform pans.

5. Place the steam rack into the Instant Pot inner pot. Add ¾ cup (180 ml) water to the inner pot. Carefully place one springform pan on top of the steam rack. (You can stack and put both in at once, but results are better when cooked separately.) Secure the lid, ensuring the valve is turned to the Sealing position. Press the Pressure Cook button and set the time to 30 minutes.

6. Once cooking is complete, turn the valve to the Venting position to release the pressure. When all the pressure is released, carefully remove the lid, holding it level to ensure that the condensed water does not fall on the cake. Remove the springform pan using oven mitts.

7. Repeat steps 5 and 6 for the second coffee cake.

8. Allow the cake to cool 5 minutes on a cooling rack. Once cool, run a knife along the insides of the springform pans to release the cakes. Remove the side of each springform pan. Slide a spatula or knife under each cake to release it from the bottom of the pan. Cut in half and serve warm. Each coffee cake serves 2.

Blueberry-Almond Crunch Coffee Cake

Yield: 4 Servings | Hands-on Time: 10 Minutes | Cooking Time: 30 Minutes |
Total Time: 45 Minutes | Buttons to Use: Pressure Cook | Release Type: Quick Release

This blueberry-speckled morning sweet is a wonderful variation of traditional coffee cake. This recipe requires two 15-ounce (450 ml) mini springform pans, 4 inches (10 cm) in diameter. For best results, cook one at a time, although it is possible to stack the pans and cook them at the same time.

FOR CAKE

4 ounces (115 g) cream cheese, room temperature

¼ cup (50 g) sugar

1 egg white

½ pint (150 g) fresh blueberries
(or ½ cup [75 g] frozen, thawed)

¾ cup (90 g) flour

1 teaspoon baking powder

½ cup (120 g) sour cream

3 tablespoons butter, melted

1 egg plus 1 egg yolk

½ teaspoon almond extract

baking spray

FOR TOPPING

½ cup (100 g) brown sugar

¼ cup (30 g) flour

2 tablespoons chilled butter, cut into small chunks

2 tablespoons sliced almonds

1. In a medium bowl, using a hand blender, combine the cream cheese, sugar, and egg white until well blended. Fold in fresh blueberries. Set aside.

2. In a medium bowl, whisk together the flour and baking powder. Add the sour cream, melted butter, egg and egg yolk, and the almond extract. Mix well with a spatula. Add the cream cheese mixture and mix well with a spatula.

3. Spray two 15-ounce (425 ml) mini springform pans with baking spray. Pour the batter evenly into the springform pans until they are three-quarters full.

4. To make the topping, combine the brown sugar and flour in a small bowl. Cut in the chilled butter chunks using two forks until the mixture is crumbly. Mix in the sliced almonds. Top each cake, dividing the topping mixture between the springform pans.

5. Place the steam rack into the Instant Pot inner pot. Add ¾ cup (180 ml) water to the inner pot. Carefully place one springform pan on top of the steam rack. (You can stack and put both in at once, but results are better when cooked separately.) Secure the lid, ensuring the valve is turned to the Sealing position. Press the Pressure Cook button and set the time to 30 minutes.

6. Once cooking is complete, turn the valve to the Venting position to release the pressure. When all the pressure is released, carefully remove the lid, holding it level to ensure that the condensed water does not fall on the cake. Remove the springform pan using oven mitts.

7. Repeat steps 5 and 6 for the second coffee cake.

8. Allow to cool 5 minutes on a cooling rack. Run a knife along the insides of the springform pans to release the cakes. Remove the side of each springform pan. Slide a spatula or knife under each cake to release it from the bottom of the pan. Cut in half and serve warm. Each coffee cake serves 2.

Coconut-Banana Steel Cut Oatmeal

Yield: 4 Servings | Hands-on Time: 5 Minutes | Cooking Time: 12 Minutes | Total Time: 30 Minutes | Buttons to Use: Pressure Cook | Release Type: Natural Release

Start your day off right with a thick, hearty, healthy bowl of oatmeal loaded with coconut flavor and topped with sliced bananas!

1 tablespoon butter

1 cup (170 g) steel cut oats

1 (15 ounce) (440 ml) can coconut milk

¼ cup (50 g) brown sugar

1 teaspoon ground cinnamon

½ teaspoon salt

sliced bananas for serving

TIP: Do not use rolled oats or quick cooking oats for this recipe or for Blueberry-Cream Steel Cut Oatmeal (page 19).

1. Put butter, oats, 2½ cups (600 ml) water, coconut milk, brown sugar, cinnamon, and salt into the Instant Pot inner pot. Mix well.

2. Secure the lid, ensuring the valve is turned to the Sealing position.

3. Press Pressure Cook and set the time to 12 minutes.

4. Once cooking is complete, allow the pot to natural release for 10 minutes. After 10 minutes, turn the valve to the Venting position to release the remaining pressure. When all the pressure is released, carefully remove the lid. Stir well. The oatmeal will thicken as it is stirred.

5. Divide the oatmeal between 4 bowls. Top each bowl with sliced bananas and serve.

Blueberry-Cream Steel Cut Oatmeal

Yield: 4 Servings | Hands-on Time: 5 Minutes | Cooking Time: 12 Minutes | Total Time: 30 Minutes |
Buttons to Use: Pressure Cook | Release Type: Natural Release

This morning cereal bursting with blueberries actually tastes like eating dessert for breakfast. Go ahead, you deserve it!

1 tablespoon butter

1 cup (170 g) steel cut oats (see Tip page 18)

1 cup (240 ml) heavy cream

1 cup (150 g) blueberries, fresh or frozen

¼ cup (50 g) sugar

½ teaspoon salt

additional blueberries for topping

1. Put butter, oats, cream, blueberries, sugar, salt, and 2 cups (480 ml) water into the Instant Pot inner pot. Mix well.

2. Secure the lid, ensuring the valve is turned to the Sealing position.

3. Press Pressure Cook and set the time to 12 minutes.

4. Once cooking is complete, allow the pot to natural release for 10 minutes. After 10 minutes, turn the valve to the Venting position to release the remaining pressure. When all the pressure is released, carefully remove the lid. Stir well. The oatmeal will thicken as it is stirred.

5. Divide the oatmeal between 4 bowls. Top each bowl with additional blueberries and serve.

Giant Oatmeal Pancake

Yield: 2 Servings | Hands-on Time: 5 Minutes | Cooking Time: 50 Minutes | Total Time: 75 Minutes |
Buttons to Use: Pressure Cook LOW PRESSURE, LESS TEMPERATURE | Release Type: No Release

This recipe yields a dense and satisfying chewy pancake that requires no flipping! It easily serves two.

½ cup (60 g) all-purpose flour

½ cup (45 g) rolled oats

2 tablespoons sugar

1½ teaspoons baking powder

¾ cup (180 ml) milk

1 egg

½ teaspoon vanilla

cooking spray or vegetable oil

butter and maple syrup for serving, if desired

1. In a medium bowl combine the flour, oats, sugar, and baking powder. Add the milk, egg, and vanilla. Mix well.

2. Thoroughly spray the Instant Pot inner pot with cooking spray, or coat with vegetable oil. Make sure the bottom is well coated.

3. Pour the batter into the prepared Instant Pot inner pot. Secure the lid, ensuring that the valve is turned to the Sealing position. Press the Pressure Cook button; then press again until the indicator light illuminates "LESS." Next, press the Pressure Level button until the "LOW" indicator is illuminated. Set the time for 40 minutes.

4. Once cooking is complete, carefully remove the lid. Remove the inner pot using oven mitts. The top of the pancake should look pale in color. The bottom will be browned.

5. Run a silicone spatula around the edge of the pancake to loosen the sides, and then work the spatula underneath the bottom of the pancake to loosen it from the inner pot. Flip the pancake out of the pot onto a plate. Cut in half to serve. Top with butter and warmed maple syrup.

NOTE: This is one of the few recipes that requires LOW PRESSURE and LESS TEMPERATURE. No pressure or steam will be released at the end of this cooking cycle because the pot will not come to full pressure.

TIP: Because this recipe requires changing the pot's pressure and temperature settings to LOW and LESS, it is important to double-check the settings the next time the pot is used. Most recipes require HIGH and NORMAL as a default.

Vanilla Yogurt

Yield: 7 Cups (1,694 g) | Hands-on Time: 5 Minutes | Cooking Time: 10 hours | Total Time: 18 hours |
Buttons to Use: Yogurt | Release Type: No Release

Yogurt in the Instant Pot is all the rage. When looking for a commercial yogurt to use as a starter, make sure it has only milk and live, active cultures as ingredients. Many brands of yogurt in the grocery store fit this category. Just read the labels. Serve the yogurt with berries and granola for a jump-start to your day.

½ gallon (1.9 L) whole milk

2 tablespoons yogurt

1 tablespoon vanilla extract (see Homemade Vanilla Extract, page 150)

fresh berries and granola for serving

TIP: It is important to have a thermometer to make yogurt. The correct temperatures for the various steps is critical to success. Also, make sure to stir the milk before checking the temperature to eliminate hot spots and get an accurate reading.

1. For best results, cool the empty Instant Pot inner pot in the refrigerator before beginning.

To Warm Milk

2. Pour cold milk into the Instant Pot inner pot. Secure the lid, ensuring the valve is turned to the Sealing position. Press the Yogurt button, and then press it again until the display says "boil." This will slowly heat the milk. The desired end temperature is 182°F (83°C). After about 25 minutes, the pot will beep, indicating that it is done.

3. Remove the lid and stir well. Measure the temperature of the milk. It should be between 180°F and 185°F (82°C to 85°C). If it is not quite up to temperature, put the lid back on and press the Yogurt button until it displays "BOIL." Check the temperature again after 5 minutes.

To Cool Milk

4. Press the Cancel button to turn the appliance off. Unplug the unit. Carefully lift the inner pot out, using oven mitts, and place on a cooling rack on the counter. Cool the milk to between 95°F and 115°F (35°C to 46°C). Stir the milk before testing the temperature. Discard any milk "skin" that has formed. To speed up this process, you can place the inner pot into a cold water bath. Just fill your sink with enough cold water to submerge the pot halfway.

Incubation

5. Once the milk has cooled to the desired temperature, place the inner pot back into the the appliance and plug in the unit. Place the yogurt in a small bowl and slowly stir in ½ cup (120 ml) of the warm milk from the inner pot. Mix well. Add the yogurt mixture to the inner pot and stir well. Secure the lid. Press the Yogurt button (you may have to press the button more than once to see the hourly timer) and adjust the time to 8 hours. For thicker yogurt, adjust the time for up to 10 hours.

6. After the set time, the display will read "Yogt" to let you know this phase is complete. The yogurt should be fairly thick. Add 1 tablespoon of vanilla and stir well. Remove the inner pot and cover the pot with plastic wrap. Place in the refrigerator to chill for 6 to 8 hours before serving.

RICE, GRAINS & PASTA

PERFECT WHITE RICE 26

CILANTRO-LIME RICE 27

HERBED RICE PILAF 28

NUTTY BROWN RICE 29

MEXICAN RICE 30

CLASSIC WHITE QUINOA 31

COLORFUL QUINOA SALAD 32

ROTINI PASTA WITH CREAMY SAUSAGE-TOMATO SAUCE 33

SPAGHETTI WITH MEAT SAUCE 34

CREAMY MAC & CHEESE 36

BEEFY MACARONI & CHEESE 37

Perfect White Rice

Yield: 4 Servings | Hands-on Time: 2 Minutes | Cooking Time: 10 Minutes | Total Time: 18 Minutes |
Buttons to Use: Rice | Release Type: Quick Release

This basic rice recipe needs to be in everyone's Instant Pot repertoire. Rinsing the rice ahead of time reduces the stickiness of the rice.

---

2 cups (360 g) long grain white rice, rinsed

1 teaspoon salt

TIP: The Rice button is a great automatic function, but it is specific to white rice. It will not work well for brown rice or wild rice, which both take more time.

1. Put rice, salt, and 2½ cups (600 ml) water into the Instant Pot inner pot and stir. Secure the lid, ensuring the valve is turned to the Sealing position. Press the Rice button. The time will automatically calculate.

2. Once cooking is complete, turn the valve to the Venting position to release the pressure. When all the pressure is released, carefully remove the lid. Fluff the rice with a fork. Add additional salt if necessary.

Cilantro-Lime Rice

Yield: 4 Servings | Hands-on Time: 5 Minutes | Cooking Time: 10 Minutes | Total Time: 20 Minutes | Buttons to Use: Rice | Release Type: Quick Release

This tangy, herby rice is great in burritos, your favorite meal-in-a-bowl by adding chicken and veggies, or as a simple side dish for any reason.

2 cups (360 g) basmati rice, rinsed well

1 teaspoon salt

1 bay leaf

¼ cup (15 g) finely chopped cilantro

2 tablespoons lime juice

1 teaspoon olive oil

zest from one lime

1. Put the rice, salt, bay leaf, and 2½ cups (600 ml) water into the Instant Pot inner pot, and stir well. Secure the lid, ensuring the valve is turned to the Sealing position. Press the Rice button. The time will automatically calculate.

2. Once cooking is complete, turn the valve to the Venting position to release the pressure. When all the pressure is released, carefully remove the lid. Fluff the rice with a fork.

3. Remove the bay leaf. Add the cilantro, lime juice, olive oil, and zest. Gently mix in with a fork. Add additional salt if necessary.

Herbed Rice Pilaf

Yield: 4 Servings | Hands-on Time: 5 Minutes | Cooking Time: 10 Minutes | Total Time: 20 Minutes |
Buttons to Use: Sauté and Rice | Release Type: Quick Release

Fresh herbs really make a difference in this dish, but dried ones can be used in a pinch. If using dried herbs, cut each measurement in half.

2 tablespoons butter

½ medium yellow onion, minced

1 cup (360) uncooked long grain white rice

1 cup (170 g) uncooked orzo pasta

3 cups (710 ml) chicken broth

½ tablespoon finely chopped fresh basil

½ tablespoon fresh thyme leaves

1 teaspoon extra virgin olive oil

TIP: Orzo is a very small pasta that can be found in nearly every grocery store. It is often mistaken for rice because its shape is similar to long grain rice.

1. Select the sauté function to heat the Instant Pot inner pot. When the display reads "Hot," add the butter. When the butter melts, add the onion and sauté for 1 to 2 minutes. Add the rice and pasta, and stir well. Sauté for another 3 minutes. Press Cancel to turn off the sauté function.

2. Add the chicken broth and stir well. Secure the lid, ensuring the valve is turned to the Sealing position. Select the Rice button. The time will automatically calculate.

3. Once cooking is complete, turn the valve to the Venting position to release the pressure. When all the pressure has released, carefully remove the lid.

4. Fluff the rice-orzo mixture with a fork. Add the basil, thyme, and olive oil. Stir and add additional salt if necessary.

Nutty Brown Rice

Yield: 4 Servings | Hands-on Time: 3 Minutes | Cooking Time: 15 Minutes | Total Time: 30 Minutes |
Buttons to Use: Sauté and Pressure Cook | Release Type: Natural Release

This nutty rice can be used in tacos, salads, or as an easy and wholesome side dish.

1 tablespoon butter

1 cup (180 g) long grain brown rice

salt as desired for taste

1. Turn on the sauté function to heat the Instant Pot inner pot. Add the butter to the inner pot. When the butter is melted, add the rice and sauté for 2 to 3 minutes.

2. Press Cancel to turn off the sauté function. Add 1½ cups (315 ml) water and stir well. Secure the lid, ensuring the valve is turned to the Sealing position. Press the Pressure Cook button and set the time to 15 minutes.

3. Once cooking is complete, allow the appliance to natural release for 10 minutes. After 10 minutes, turn the valve to the Venting position to release the pressure. When all the pressure is released, carefully remove the lid. Fluff the rice with a fork and add salt as desired.

Mexican Rice

Yield: 4 Servings | Hands-on Time: 5 Minutes | Cooking Time: 10 Minutes | Total Time: 20 Minutes |
Buttons to Use: Sauté and Rice | Release Type: Quick Release

Sautéing white rice with onion, garlic, and tomato paste gives this rice a rich, deep flavor. Serve with your favorite south-of-the-border entree, like Cheesy Chicken Salsa Verde (page 54).

1 tablespoon olive oil

½ medium onion, minced

1 clove garlic, minced

2 cups (360 g) uncooked white rice

2 tablespoons tomato paste

2 cups (480 ml) broth, chicken or vegetable

1 (8-ounce) (225 g) jar salsa of your choice

1. Turn on the sauté function to heat the Instant Pot inner pot. Once it is hot, coat the bottom of the inner pot with olive oil. Add the onion and garlic, and sauté for 3 minutes, stirring continuously. Add the rice and tomato paste and stir well. Sauté for an additional 2 minutes.

2. Press Cancel to turn off the sauté function. Add the broth and salsa to the rice mixture. Stir well. Secure the lid, ensuring the valve is turned to the Sealing position. Press the Rice button. The time will automatically calculate.

3. Once cooking is complete, turn the valve to the Venting position to release the pressure. When all the pressure is released, carefully remove the lid. Fluff the rice with a fork before serving.

Classic White Quinoa

Yield: 4 Servings | Hands-on Time: 2 Minutes | Cooking Time: 10 minutes | Total Time: 15 Minutes |
Buttons to Use: Rice | Release Type: Quick Release

These mighty seeds have a bit of bite and are loaded with 8 grams of protein per cup. With all 9 essential amino acids, quinoa is considered a complete protein. Use it as you would rice or any other cooked grain.

2 cups (360 g) white quinoa, rinsed

2 cups (480 ml) chicken or vegetable broth

1 teaspoon salt

1. Add all the ingredients to Instant Pot inner pot and stir well. Secure the lid, ensuring the valve is turned to the Sealing position. Press the Rice button. The time will automatically calculate.

2. Once cooking is complete, turn the valve to the Venting position to release the pressure. When all the pressure is released, carefully remove the lid. Fluff the quinoa with a fork and serve immediately.

Colorful Quinoa Salad

Yield: 4 Servings | Hands-on Time: 15 Minutes | Cooking Time: 10 Minutes | Total Time: 35 Minutes |
Buttons to Use: Rice | Release Type: Quick Release

This salad has it all! It's a fresh, healthy, and delicious meatless meal or a tasty accompaniment to your favorite entrée.

FOR THE SALAD

1 cup (180 g) dry tri-colored quinoa, rinsed (or white quinoa)

1 cup (240 ml) chicken broth

½ teaspoon salt

1 cup (45 g) chopped baby kale

1 pint (275 g) cherry tomatoes, sliced in half

1 cucumber, sliced and quartered

4 radishes, thinly sliced

3 green onions, white and light-green parts, sliced

FOR THE DRESSING

½ cup (120 ml) extra virgin olive oil

¼ cup (60 ml) white wine vinegar

½ teaspoon dried thyme

½ teaspoon dried oregano

½ teaspoon dried basil

½ teaspoon salt

¼ teaspoon pepper

1. Put the quinoa, broth, and salt in the Instant Pot inner pot and stir well. Secure the lid, ensuring the valve is turned to the Sealing position. Press the Rice button. The time will automatically calculate.

2. Once cooking is complete, turn the valve to the Venting position to release the pressure. When all the pressure is released, carefully remove the lid. Fluff the quinoa with a fork and set aside to cool.

3. In a large bowl, combine the kale, tomatoes, cucumber, radishes, green onions, and cooled quinoa. Toss to mix well.

4. In a small bowl, combine all the dressing ingredients and whisk together. Drizzle dressing on top of the salad and toss to combine.

Rotini Pasta with Creamy Sausage-Tomato Sauce

Yield: 4 Servings | Hands-on Time: 10 Minutes | Cooking Time: 5 Minutes | Total Time: 20 Minutes |
Buttons to Use: Sauté and Pressure Cook | Release Type: Quick Release

With a quick splash of cream at the end of the recipe, this flavorful pasta dish with spicy sausage is easy to pull together on the fly.

1 tablespoon extra virgin olive oil

½ medium onion, diced

1 pound (450 g) ground hot Italian sausage

1 teaspoon salt

½ teaspoon pepper

1 teaspoon Italian seasoning

1 (15-ounce) (425 g) can diced tomatoes, not drained

8 ounces (225 g) rotini pasta

½ cup (120 ml) cream

1. Select the sauté function to heat the Instant Pot inner pot. Once the display reads "Hot," add the oil to coat the bottom of the pot. Add the onion and sausage, stirring until the sausage is crumbly and no longer pink. Press Cancel to turn off the sauté function.

2. Add salt, pepper, Italian seasoning, tomatoes, and 2 cups (480 ml) water. Stir well. Add the pasta and stir lightly to submerge pasta. Secure the lid, ensuring valve is turned to the Sealing position. Press the Pressure Cook button and set the time to 5 minutes.

3. Once cooking is complete, turn the valve to the Venting position to release all the pressure. When all the pressure is released, carefully remove the lid.

4. Add the cream and stir well. The sauce will thicken upon standing.

Spaghetti with Meat Sauce

Yield: 4 Servings | Hands-on Time: 15 Minutes | Cooking Time: 4 Minutes | Total Time: 25 Minutes |
Buttons to Use: Sauté and Pressure Cook | Release Type: Quick Release

This recipe may well be the definitive one-pot meal. Healthy, homemade, and heart-warming spaghetti with meat sauce makes a great weeknight family meal and gets even better with only one pot to clean!

1 tablespoon olive oil

½ medium onion, chopped

2 cloves garlic, minced

1 pound (450 g) lean ground beef

1 (15-ounce) (425 g) can crushed tomatoes

1 (4-ounce) (115 g) can tomato paste

1 tablespoon oregano

1 tablespoon basil

¼ teaspoon red pepper flakes

8 ounces (225 g) uncooked spaghetti, broken in half

grated Parmesan cheese for serving

fresh basil for serving

1. Select the sauté function to heat the Instant Pot inner pot. Once the display reads "Hot," coat the bottom of the pan with olive oil. Add the onion and sauté for approximately 3 minutes until slightly soft and translucent. Mix in the garlic and sauté for another minute. Add the ground beef and cook until the meat is brown, stirring to break into crumbles.

2. Stir in the crushed tomatoes, tomato paste, oregano, basil, and red pepper flakes until well combined. Add 3 cups (710 ml) water and mix well.

3. Fan out the spaghetti (broken in half) across the top of the sauce mixture. Press the spaghetti down until slightly submerged, approximately 1 inch (2.5 cm) below the surface of the liquid.

4. Press the Cancel button to turn off the sauté function. Secure the lid, ensuring the valve is turned to the Sealing position. Press the Pressure Cook button and set the time to 4 minutes.

5. Once cooking is complete, turn the valve to the Venting position to release the pressure. When all the pressure is released, carefully remove the lid. Stir the pasta with a spaghetti lifter or large fork, separating any pasta that may have stuck together. Divide spaghetti between four bowls and top with Parmesan cheese and basil, if desired.

Creamy Mac & Cheese

Yield: 4 Servings | Hands-on Time: 5 Minutes | Cooking Time: 5 Minutes | Total Time: 20 Minutes | Buttons to Use: Sauté and Pressure Cook | Release Type: Quick Release

This, cheesy and comforting pasta dish will remind you of the stovetop favorite and make a frequent appearance at the dinner table.

4 tablespoons butter

¼ cup (30 g) flour

2 cups (480 ml) whole milk

1 cup (240 ml) cream

1 (10½-ounce) (320 ml) can condensed cream of Cheddar soup

½ teaspoon dry mustard

½ teaspoon pepper

½ teaspoon salt

1 (8-ounce) (225 g) box of small elbow macaroni, uncooked

3 cups (345 g) shredded sharp Cheddar cheese, preferably freshly shredded from the block

½ cup (50 g) shredded Parmesan cheese for serving

1. Select the sauté function to heat the Instant Pot inner pot. Once the display reads "Hot," add the butter. As soon as the butter melts, mix in the flour and stir to form a thick paste, or roux. Stir continuously until the roux turns golden, and then slowly whisk in 1 cup (240 ml) water to thin the paste. With a spatula, scrape any browned bits off the bottom of pan. Press Cancel to turn off the sauté function.

2. Add the milk, cream, soup, dry mustard, pepper, and salt. Stir in macaroni.

3. Secure the lid, ensuring the valve is turned to the Sealing position. Press the Pressure Cook button and set the time to 5 minutes.

4. Once cooking is complete, turn the valve to the Venting position to release the pressure. When all the pressure is released, carefully remove the lid. Stir the macaroni and gradually add the shredded cheese, stirring until fully melted. Serve sprinkled with Parmesan cheese, if desired.

Beefy Macaroni & Cheese

Yield: 4 Servings | Hands-on Time: 10 Minutes | Cooking Time: 5 Minutes | Total Time: 20 Minutes |
Buttons to Use: Sauté and Pressure Cook | Release Type: Quick Release

Beefy Macaroni & Cheese is an all-around family favorite. Make sure to use lean ground beef to avoid having to drain the fat off after sautéing.

2 tablespoons butter

1 pound (450 g) 93% lean ground beef

½ teaspoon salt

½ teaspoon pepper

½ teaspoon dry mustard

½ teaspoon onion powder

1 (10½-ounce) (320 ml) can condensed cream of Cheddar soup

1 cup (240 ml) milk

8 ounces (225 g) uncooked elbow macaroni

8 ounces shredded Cheddar cheese

1. Select the sauté function to heat the Instant Pot inner pot. Once the display reads "Hot," add the butter. When the butter melts, add the ground beef, salt, pepper, dry mustard, and onion powder. Brown the beef until no longer pink, stirring to break it into bite-size crumbles.

2. Press Cancel to turn off the sauté function. Pour in the soup and milk. Stir well.

3. Add the macaroni. Pour 2 cups (480 ml) water on top and stir until combined. Secure the lid, ensuring the valve is turned to the Sealing position. Press the Pressure Cook button and set the time to 5 minutes.

4. Once cooking is complete, turn the valve to the Venting position to let the pressure release. When all the pressure is released, carefully remove the lid. Stir and gradually add the shredded cheese, stirring until fully melted.

BEANS

BLACK BEANS WITH GARLIC & ONION 40

PINTO BEANS 41

REFRIED BEANS 42

WHITE BEANS WITH TOMATILLO SALSA 43

LENTILS WITH HAM 44

BLACK-EYED PEAS 45

RED BEANS & RICE WITH ANDOUILLE SAUSAGE 46

HOMEMADE HUMMUS 48

Black Beans with Garlic & Onion

Yield: 4 Servings | Hands-on Time: 5 Minutes | Cooking Time: 30 Minutes | Total Time: 45 Minutes |
Buttons to Use: Bean/Chili | Release Type: Natural Release

Transforming dry beans to plump ones is one of the most useful functions of the Instant Pot. Plus, no soaking is required!

1 pound (450 g) dry black beans, rinsed well

2 cloves garlic, peeled and smashed

½ medium onion, finely chopped

1 tablespoon vegetable oil

1 teaspoon salt

1. Add dry ingredients and 5 cups (1,180 ml) water to the Instant Pot inner pot and stir well. Secure the lid, ensuring the valve is turned to the Sealing position. Press the Bean/Chili button and set the time to 30 minutes.

2. Once cooking is complete, allow the appliance to natural release for 10 minutes and then turn the valve to the Venting position to release the remaining pressure.

3. When all the pressure is released, carefully remove the lid and stir well. Serve immediately, or pour the contents into a colander to remove juice, and serve.

Pinto Beans

Yield: 4–6 Servings | Hands-on Time: 5 Minutes | Cooking Time: 45 Minutes | Total Time: 75 Minutes | Buttons to Use: Pressure Cook | Release Type: Natural Release

These amazing Instant Pot beans are perfectly tender and ready in less than 90 minutes. After rinsing, make sure to remove any beans that are cracked or deformed. Serve as a side dish or in any of your favorite recipes with pinto beans.

1 pound (450 g) dry pinto beans, rinsed, but not soaked

1 well-rinsed ham hock (optional)

1 bay leaf

1 tablespoon vegetable oil

TIP: The vegetable oil is an important ingredient in this dish. It prevents the beans from foaming up and clogging the pressure release valve during the cooking process.

1. Add the beans, ham hock, bay leaf, and 6 cups (1,420 ml) water to the Instant Pot inner pot. Mix well. Add the oil.

2. Secure the lid, ensuring the valve is turned to the Sealing position. Press the Pressure Cook button and set the time to 45 minutes.

3. Once cooking is complete, allow the appliance to natural release for 20 minutes and then turn the valve to the Venting position to release the remaining pressure. When all the pressure is released, carefully remove the lid. Transfer the ham hock and beans to a serving bowl using a slotted spoon.

Refried Beans

Yield: 4 Servings | Hands-on Time: 5 Minutes | Cooking Time: 60 Minutes | Total Time: 90 Minutes |
Buttons to Use: Bean/Chili | Release Type: Natural Release

There's nothing quite like homemade refried beans. Leave out the jalapeño if you don't prefer the extra kick.

1 cup (140 g) dried pinto beans, rinsed but not soaked

1 jalapeño, seeded and minced

2 cloves garlic, peeled and smashed

1 tablespoon olive oil

1 teaspoon salt

1 bay leaf

1 jalapeño, sliced for serving (optional)

1. Put all the dry ingredients and 4 cups (950 ml) water in the Instant Pot inner pot and stir well.

2. Press the Bean/Chili button and secure the lid, ensuring the valve is turned to the Sealing position. Set the time to 60 minutes.

3. Once cooking is complete, allow the appliance to natural release for 15 minutes. After 15 minutes, turn the valve to the Venting position to release the pressure. When all the pressure is released, carefully remove the lid.

4. Place a colander in a large bowl. Drain the contents of the pot into the colander, reserving the juice. Remove the bay leaf.

5. Pour the beans back into the inner pot. Add ½ cup (120 ml) reserved bean juice and, using an immersion blender, blend until smooth, adding additional liquid if needed. (This step can also be done in a blender or food processor.)

6. Once the beans have reached the desired consistency, add additional salt to taste, and mix well. Top with sliced jalapeño and serve.

White Beans with Tomatillo Salsa

Yield: 6 Servings | Hands-on Time: 2 Minutes | Cooking Time: 45 Minutes | Total Time: 40 Minutes | Buttons to Use: Bean/Chili | Release Type: Natural Release

Cannellini and great northern beans are the most common types of white beans, and either will work well in this recipe.

1 pound (450 g) dry white beans (cannellini or great northern), well rinsed

1 (16-ounce) (450 g) jar tomatillo salsa

1 teaspoon salt

1 tablespoon vegetable oil

1. Put all the ingredients plus 4 cups (950 ml) water into the Instant Pot inner pot and stir well. Secure the lid, ensuring the valve is turned to the Sealing position. Press the Bean/Chili button and set the time to 45 minutes.

2. Once cooking is complete, allow the appliance to natural release for 15 minutes. After 15 minutes, turn the valve to the Venting position to release the pressure. When all the pressure is released, carefully remove the lid and stir. Serve as a side dish, or use in other entrées.

Lentils with Ham

Yield: 4 Servings | Hands-on Time: 5 Minutes | Cooking Time: 15 Minutes | Total Time: 25 Minutes |
Buttons to Use: Pressure Cook | Release Type: Quick Release

This classic dish is a wonderful combination that has withstood the test of time. Consider this recipe when you have leftover smoky, salty ham and need a quick, satisfying weeknight meal.

1 cup (130 g) dried green or brown lentils

1 pound (450 g) cooked ham, cut into bite-sized chunks

½ medium onion, chopped

1 clove garlic, minced

2 tablespoons butter

1 bay leaf

1½ cups (360 ml) vegetable broth (or water)

1. Put all ingredients into the Instant Pot inner pot and stir. Secure the lid, ensuring the valve is turned to the Sealing position. Press Pressure Cook and set the time to 15 minutes.

2. Once cooking is complete, turn the valve to the Venting position to release the pressure. When all the pressure is released, carefully remove the lid and stir. Remove the bay leaf. Add salt to taste, if needed before serving.

TIP: If you have any leftover greens like kale or collard greens in the fridge, toss them in!

Black-Eyed Peas

Yield: 4 Servings | Hands-on Time: 10 Minutes | Cooking Time: 25 Minutes | Total Time: 45 Minutes | Buttons to Use: Bean/Chili | Release Type: Natural Release

Black-eyed peas are often served during a celebration such as New Year's Day. And cooked in less than an hour—that's worth raving about, too!

---

1 pound (450 g) dry black-eyed peas, rinsed well

1 bay leaf

1 teaspoon salt

1 tablespoon vegetable oil

1. Add all ingredients plus 5 cups (1,180 ml) water to the Instant Pot inner pot and stir well. Secure the lid, ensuring the valve is turned to the Sealing position. Select the Bean/Chili button and set the time to 25 minutes.

2. Once cooking is complete, allow the appliance to natural release for 10 minutes. After 10 minutes, turn the valve to the Venting position to release the pressure.

3. When all the pressure is released, carefully remove the lid and stir well. Remove the bay leaf. Transfer the black-eyed peas to a bowl using a slotted spoon and serve as a side dish, or use in your favorite recipe.

Red Beans & Rice with Andouille Sausage

Yield: 6 Servings | Hands-on Time: 10 Minutes | Cooking Time: 60 Minutes | Total Time: 90 Minutes |
Buttons to Use: Rice and Pressure Cook | Release Type: Natural Release

A Cajun favorite comfort food, this recipe is made in two easy steps and makes for great leftovers.

RICE

1 cup (180 g) uncooked white rice

½ teaspoon salt

chopped parsley, for garnish

RED BEANS & SAUSAGE

1 cup (150 g) dried red beans

1 pound (450 g) cooked andouille sausage, sliced

2 stalks celery, sliced

1 medium green bell pepper, seeded and diced

½ medium onion, diced

1 clove garlic, minced

1 teaspoon dried oregano

1 teaspoon salt

½ teaspoon cayenne pepper

Prepare Rice

1. Add the rice, salt, and 1½ cups (360 ml) water to the Instant Pot inner pot and stir. Secure the lid, ensuring the valve is turned to the Sealing position. Select the Rice button. The timer will self-calculate.

2. Once cooking is complete, turn the valve to the Venting position to release the pressure. When all the pressure is released, carefully remove the lid. Fluff the rice with a fork. Transfer the rice to a large bowl, garnish with parsley, and set aside. Wash and dry the inner pot.

Prepare Red Beans & Sausage

3. Add all the remaining ingredients plus 3 cups (710 ml) water to the inner pot and stir well. Secure the lid, ensuring the valve is turned to the Sealing position. Press the Pressure Cook button and set the time to 45 minutes.

4. Once cooking is complete, allow the appliance to natural release for 10 minutes. After 10 minutes, turn the valve to the Venting position to release the pressure.

5. When all the pressure is released, carefully remove the lid and stir well. Serve the bean/sausage mixture and rice either separately or combined.

Homemade Hummus

Yield: 4 cups | Hands-on Time: 5 Minutes | Cooking Time: 50 Minutes | Total Time: 75 Minutes |
Buttons to Use: Bean/Chili | Release Type: Natural Release

Although readily available at the supermarket, hummus is very economical to make at home. This recipe requires a food processor or blender.

2 cups (360 g) dried chickpeas (also called garbanzo beans)

3 garlic cloves, peeled and smashed

1 tablespoon vegetable oil

1 teaspoon salt

½ teaspoon pepper

⅓ cup (80 ml) olive oil, divided and plus extra to serve

pita bread, carrots, peppers, cucumbers for serving

TIP: To try different hummus flavors, consider adding roasted red peppers, hot pepper sauce, or fresh herbs during the blending phase.

1. Place the chickpeas and the garlic in the Instant Pot inner pot. Add 5 cups (1,180 ml) water and stir. Add the vegetable oil. Secure the lid, ensuring the valve is turned to the Sealing position. Press the Bean/Chili button and set the time to 50 minutes.

2. Once cooking is complete, allow the appliance to natural release for 10 minutes. After 10 minutes, turn the valve to the Venting position to release the pressure.

3. When all the pressure is released, carefully remove the lid. Place a colander over a large bowl in the sink. Drain the chickpeas into the colander and capture the chickpea cooking liquid in the bowl, reserving the liquid for later use.

4. Once drained, combine the chickpeas with salt, pepper, 3 tablespoons olive oil, and ¼ cup (60 ml) of the reserved chickpea liquid in a food processor. If using a blender, this step will need to be done in two batches. Pulse the food processor to blend the ingredients. Then turn the food processor to high, slowly adding the remaining olive oil and reserved chickpea cooking liquid as needed until smooth and of the desired consistency. Before serving, place in a bowl, drizzle additional olive oil on top, and season with freshly cracked black pepper. Serve with pita bread, carrots, peppers, and cucumbers.

MEAT & POULTRY

CHICKEN & DUMPLINGS *52*

CHEESY CHICKEN SALSA VERDE *54*

CRACK CHICKEN *55*

WEEKNIGHT GUMBO *56*

CHEESY CHICKEN & RICE *58*

HUNTER CHICKEN *60*

SHREDDED BBQ BEEF SANDWICHES *62*

TOASTED CHEESESTEAK SANDWICHES *63*

MISSISSIPPI POT ROAST *64*

MONGOLIAN BEEF *66*

BEEFY CREAMY POTATOES AU GRATIN *68*

GROUND BEEF STROGANOFF *70*

FRESH SALMON WITH LEMON & DILL *71*

TANGY SLOPPY JOES *72*

BBQ BABY BACK RIBS *73*

SWEET & SPICY ASIAN RIBS *74*

HAWAIIAN SHREDDED PORK *76*

BEER-BRAISED SHREDDED PORK *78*

PORK LOIN ROAST *80*

PORK CHOPS SMOTHERED WITH ONIONS *82*

Chicken & Dumplings

Yield: 4 Servings | Hands-on Time: 10 Minutes | Cooking Time: 8 Minutes | Total Time: 30 Minutes |
Buttons to Use: Sauté and Pressure Cook | Release Type: Natural Release

Chicken and dumplings is one of the quintessential comfort foods. This recipe uses prepared biscuits, but use your own homemade biscuit recipe if you prefer.

1 tablespoon olive oil

2 medium carrots, sliced

3 stalks celery, sliced

½ medium onion, chopped

1 pound (450 g) chicken tenders, cut into 2-inch (5 cm) pieces

½ cup (60 g) flour

1 teaspoon thyme

½ teaspoon salt

¼ teaspoon pepper

2 cups (480 ml) chicken broth

1 can refrigerated biscuits, uncooked. (You will only use 5 for this recipe, so bake the other 3 according to package directions to have a few extra on hand.)

¼ cup (60 ml) heavy cream

1 cup (135 g) frozen peas, thawed

1. Turn on the sauté function to heat up the Instant Pot inner pot. Coat the bottom with olive oil. When hot, add the carrots, celery, and onion and sauté for 3 to 4 minutes, or until the onions are translucent.

2. Add the chicken and stir well. Sprinkle with flour and stir continuously until the chicken and vegetable mixture is well coated. Mix in the thyme, salt, pepper, and chicken broth. Stir well, making sure to scrape the bottom clean of brown bits.

3. Cut 5 biscuits into quarters. Drop the biscuit pieces on top of the chicken mixture. Do not stir or submerge.

4. Press Cancel to turn off the sauté function. Secure the lid, ensuring the valve is turned to the Sealing position. Press the Pressure Cook button and set the time to 8 minutes.

5. Once cooking is complete, allow the appliance to natural release for 10 minutes. After 10 minutes, turn the valve to the Venting position to release the pressure.

6. When the pressure is released, carefully remove the lid. Stir in the cream and peas. Divide among 4 bowls and serve.

Cheesy Chicken Salsa Verde

Yield: 4 Servings | Hands-on Time: 5 Minutes | Cooking Time: 25 Minutes | Total Time: 35 Minutes |
Buttons to Use: Pressure Cook | Release Type: Quick Release

This warm, gooey, shredded chicken dish makes a great filling in tacos or over Cilantro-Lime Rice (page 27). Serve with desired toppings such as salsa, sour cream, or veggies.

1 pound (450 g) boneless, skinless chicken thighs

8 ounces (225 g) jarred or homemade salsa verde

salt and pepper to taste

1 tablespoon cornstarch

8 ounces (225 g) shredded Pepper Jack cheese

corn tortillas, warmed

1. Place the chicken thighs in the Instant Pot inner pot. Pour the salsa on top of the chicken, ensuring the meat is covered. Secure the lid, ensuring the valve is turned to the Sealing position. Press the Pressure Cook button and set the time to 25 minutes.

2. Once cooking is complete, turn the valve to the Venting position to release the pressure. Press the Cancel button to turn off the appliance. When the pressure is released, carefully remove the lid.

3. Remove the chicken and place it into a medium bowl. Using two forks, shred the chicken. Add salt and pepper to taste.

4. In a small bowl combine the cornstarch and 1 tablespoon water. Press the Sauté button and stir the cornstarch mixture into the liquid in the inner pot. Whisk until the sauce simmers and thickens slightly. Add the cheese to the sauce one handful at a time, stirring constantly, until all the cheese is melted and well incorporated. Add the chicken back to the pot and stir well. Serve with tortillas.

Crack Chicken

Yield: 4 Servings | Hands-on Time: 10 Minutes | Cooking Time: 12 Minutes | Total Time: 30 Minutes |
Buttons to Use: Sauté and Pressure Cook | Release Type: Natural Release

One of the most popular Instant Pot recipes on the Internet, this chicken dish should come with an addiction warning. Serve with crackers or toasted bread of choice.

12 ounces (340 g) bacon, sliced crosswise into bite-sized pieces.

1 pound (450 g) boneless, skinless chicken breasts

1 packet (1-ounce) (28 g) dry ranch dressing

4 ounces (115 g) cream cheese, room temperature and cut into bite-sized chunks

1 cup (240 ml) chicken broth

1 cup (115 g) shredded Cheddar cheese

2 green onions, sliced crosswise for serving

1. Select the sauté function to heat the Instant Pot inner pot. When the display reads "Hot," add the bacon. Sauté the bacon, stirring occasionally, until crisp. Press Cancel to turn off the sauté function. Transfer the bacon to a paper towel–lined plate using a slotted spoon. Drain the bacon grease from the inner pot into a heat-proof receptacle for disposal.

2. Reserve 2 tablespoons of crisp bacon for serving and return the remaining bacon to the inner pot. Add the chicken, ranch dressing, cream cheese, and chicken broth. Secure the lid, ensuring the valve is turned to the Sealing position. Press the Pressure Cook button and set the time to 12 minutes.

3. Once cooking is complete, allow the appliance to natural release for 5 minutes. After 5 minutes, turn the valve to the Venting position to release the pressure.

4. When all the pressure is released, carefully remove the lid. Using tongs, remove the chicken and place in a bowl. Using two forks, shred the chicken. Whisk together the sauce remaining in the pot. When the cream cheese is fully incorporated, return the chicken to the pot and stir well.

5. Pour the mixture into a serving dish and top with reserved bacon, shredded cheese, and green onion.

Weeknight Gumbo

Yield: 4 Servings | Hands-on Time: 15 Minutes | Cooking Time: 15 Minutes | Total Time: 40 Minutes |
Buttons to Use: Sauté and Pressure Cook | Release Type: Natural Release

For a taste of New Orleans, stir up this spicy stew with andouille sausage and chicken. Adjust the heat level by decreasing the creole seasoning and cayenne pepper, if preferred.

---

4 tablespoons butter

2 tablespoons olive oil

½ cup (60 g) flour

2 teaspoons creole seasoning

2 teaspoons Worcestershire sauce

1 teaspoon smoked paprika

½ teaspoon dried basil

½ teaspoon cayenne pepper

½ teaspoon dried thyme

1 teaspoon salt

4 cups (950 ml) chicken broth (bone broth is best)

2 stalks celery, sliced crosswise into bite-sized pieces

1 medium green bell pepper, seeded and diced

½ medium onion, diced

8 ounces (225 g) boneless, skinless chicken thighs, cut into bite-sized pieces

8 ounces (225 g) andouille sausage, sliced into thin discs

juice from one lime

cooked rice for serving

1. Select the sauté function to heat the Instant Pot inner pot. Add the butter and olive oil. When the butter melts, add the flour and stir constantly to prevent burning, approximately five minutes until golden brown. Add the creole seasoning, Worcestershire sauce, paprika, basil, cayenne pepper, thyme, and salt. Continue to stir constantly until the mixture turns light golden brown.

2. Press Cancel to turn off the sauté function. Add the chicken broth to deglaze the pot, scraping all brown bits off the bottom of the pot with a wooden spoon. Whisk to blend well.

3. Add the celery, bell pepper, onion, chicken, and sausage to the inner pot. Stir and secure the lid, ensuring the valve is turned to the Sealing position. Press the Pressure Cook button and set the time to 15 minutes.

4. Once cooking is complete, allow the appliance to natural release for 10 minutes. After 10 minutes, turn the valve to the Venting position to release the remaining pressure. When all the pressure is released, carefully remove the lid. Add the lime juice and additional salt to taste. Place rice in the bottom of each of 4 bowls. Divide the gumbo evenly among the bowls and serve.

NOTE: If you want a thicker soup base after all of the ingredients have been added, mix 2 tablespoons cornstarch with 2 tablespoons water and add to the pot. Select the sauté function and stir until the soup bubbles and starts to thicken. Turn off the sauté function by pressing Cancel.)

TIP: The flour and butter mixture created at the beginning of the recipe is called a roux. After making the roux, it is important to deglaze the bottom of the pot to make sure browned bits of food are not stuck to the pot. Stuck food bits can interfere with pressurization.

Cheesy Chicken & Rice

Yield: 4 Servings | Hands-on Time: 15 Minutes | Cooking Time: 5 Minutes | Total Time: 30 Minutes |
Buttons to Use: Sauté and Pressure Cook | Release Type: Quick Release

Combine tender chicken, velvety Cheddar, and starchy rice in one pot for an easy weeknight meal sure to please all.

2 tablespoons butter

½ medium onion, diced

1 clove garlic, minced

1 pound (450 g) chicken tenders, cut into bite-sized pieces

1 teaspoon salt

½ teaspoon pepper

1 cup (180 g) uncooked long grain white rice

1¼ cup (300 ml) chicken broth

1 tablespoon cornstarch

¼ cup (60 ml) whole milk

1 cup (115 g) shredded sharp Cheddar cheese

1 cup (135 g) frozen peas, thawed

1. Select the sauté function to heat the Instant Pot inner pot. Add butter. When the butter is melted, mix in the onion and garlic, and sauté until the onion becomes translucent. Add the chicken, salt and pepper. Continue to sauté an additional 5 minutes until the chicken begins to brown. Press Cancel to turn off the sauté function.

2. Add rice and chicken broth to the inner pot and stir. Secure the lid, ensuring the valve is turned to the Sealing position. Press the Pressure Cook button and set the time to 5 minutes.

3. In a small bowl, whisk together the cornstarch and milk. Set aside.

4. Once cooking is complete, turn the valve to the Venting position to release the pressure. When all the pressure is released, carefully remove the lid and press Cancel to turn off the Instant Pot.

5. Press the Sauté button and add the cornstarch mixture. Stir continuously until the sauce begins to thicken. Add the shredded cheese one handful at a time and stir well until all cheese is melted and incorporated.

6. Add peas, stir, and serve immediately.

TIP: Freshly shredded cheese right from the block will melt much better than pre-shredded due to the preservatives manufacturers add to pre-shredded cheese.

Hunter Chicken

Yield: 4 Servings | Hands-on Time: 10 Minutes | Cooking Time: 20 Minutes | Total Time: 40 Minutes |
Buttons to Use: Sauté and Pressure Cook | Release Type: Quick Release

The secret to tender, juicy meat? Use bone-in, skin-on chicken thighs. Serve this tangy poultry dish with glutinous polenta to soak up all the wonderful juices.

1 tablespoon vegetable oil

½ medium onion, sliced

8 ounces (225 g) sliced mushrooms

2 cloves garlic, peeled and minced

¼ cup (60 ml) red wine (optional, or substitute with water or chicken broth)

3 pounds (1.35 kg) bone-in, skin-on chicken thighs or quarters

1 can diced tomatoes with juice, 28 ounces (800 g)

½ teaspoon salt

½ teaspoon pepper

1 teaspoon dried oregano

1 teaspoon dried thyme

1 teaspoon dried rosemary

1. Select the sauté function to heat the Instant Pot inner pot. When the display reads "Hot," add the oil and heat until shimmering. Add the onion, mushrooms, and garlic, and sauté, stirring continuously, until mushrooms start to release their juices, approximately 5 minutes. Add the wine to deglaze the bottom of the inner pot, scraping up all the browned bits stuck to the bottom.

2. Lay the chicken, skin side down, on top of mushroom mixture. Press Cancel to turn off the sauté function.

3. Add the tomatoes, salt, pepper, oregano, thyme, rosemary, and ½ cup (120 ml) water. Stir to combine. Secure the lid, ensuring the valve is turned to the Sealing position. Press the Pressure Cook button and set the time to 20 minutes.

4. Once cooking is complete, turn the valve to the Venting position to release the pressure. When all the pressure is released, carefully open the lid and stir gently to combine the ingredients. Remove the chicken using tongs and set on a serving platter. Pour the sauce over the chicken and serve with polenta.

Shredded BBQ Beef Sandwiches

Yield: 4 Servings | Hands-on Time: 5 Minutes | Cooking Time: 60 Minutes | Total Time: 80 Minutes |
Buttons to Use: Pressure Cook | Release Type: Natural Release

Get restaurant-quality barbecue sandwiches on your table in less than 90 minutes. It will taste like it cooked for hours!

3 pounds (1.35 kg) chuck roast, cut into 4- to 5-inch (about 10 to 12 cm) pieces

1 medium onion, sliced

3 cloves garlic, peeled and smashed

8 ounces (225 g) barbecue sauce of choice

1 tablespoon cornstarch

sandwich buns

1. Place the chuck roast, onion, garlic, barbecue sauce, and ¾ cup (180 ml) water into the Instant Pot inner pot. Secure the lid, ensuring the valve is turned to the Sealing position. Press the Pressure Cook button and set the time to 60 minutes.

2. Once cooking is complete, allow the appliance to natural release for 15 minutes. After 15 minutes, turn the valve to the Venting position to release the pressure. Press Cancel to turn off the appliance.

3. When all the pressure is released, carefully remove the lid and transfer the beef to a large bowl. Using two forks, shred the beef. Set aside.

4. Press the Sauté button to heat the leftover liquid in the inner pot. As the liquid heats, combine the cornstarch and 1 tablespoon water in a small bowl. When the liquid begins to bubble, whisk in the cornstarch mixture. Continue whisking until the sauce thickens. Return the beef to the pot and stir until well coated with sauce.

5. Serve the shredded barbecue beef on toasted buns. Drizzle extra sauce on top of the beef as desired.

Toasted Cheesesteak Sandwiches

Yield: 4 Servings | Hands-on Time: 5 Minutes | Cooking Time: 4 Minutes | Total Time: 15 Minutes |
Buttons to Use: Pressure Cook | Release Type: Quick Release

After assembling this sliced strip steak sandwich, place it under the broiler in your oven for a few moments to melt the Provolone cheese. This recipe also uses the broiler in your oven.

1 tablespoon butter

1 medium green bell pepper, seeded and sliced

1 medium onion, sliced

½ teaspoon salt

¼ teaspoon pepper

2 pounds (900 g) strip steak, thinly sliced against the grain

4 hoagie rolls, sliced lengthwise

4 slices Provolone cheese

1. Select the sauté function to heat the Instant Pot inner pot. When the pot displays "Hot," add the butter. When the butter is melted, add the bell pepper, onion, salt, and pepper. Sauté until the onion becomes translucent.

2. Press Cancel to turn off the sauté function. Add the steak and stir to combine. Secure the lid, ensuring the valve is turned to the Sealing position. Press the Pressure Cook button and set the time to 4 minutes.

3. Once cooking is complete, turn the valve to the Venting position to release the pressure. When all the pressure is released, carefully remove the lid.

4. Turn on the broiler. Open hoagie rolls, and place them on a baking sheet. Evenly divide the beef mixture on top of one side of each hoagie roll. Top each sandwich with a slice of cheese, covering the beef completely.

5. Place the baking sheet approximately 4 inches (10 cm) below the broiler. Toast the sandwiches, removing them when the cheese begins to melt, approximately 5 minutes. Fold the sandwiches closed and serve immediately.

Mississippi Pot Roast

Yield: 4 Servings | Hands-on Time: 15 Minutes | Cooking Time: 45 Minutes | Total Time: 90 Minutes |
Buttons to Use: Sauté and Meat/Stew | Release Type: Natural Release

The most unpredictably delicious roast you will ever eat. With minimal and inexpensive ingredients this slow cooked Internet sensation can be done in a fraction of the time in the Instant Pot. Don't skip the pepperoncinis—they help cut through the meaty flavor when cooking this dish.

2 tablespoons olive oil

1 chuck roast, 3 pounds (1.35 kg)

4 tablespoons butter

1 (1-ounce) (28 g) packet dry au jus mix

1 (1-ounce) (28 g) packet dry ranch dressing mix

4 to 8 pepperoncinis, depending on personal taste for spice

1 tablespoon cornstarch

additional pepperoncinis for serving

chopped parsley for serving

1. Select the sauté function to heat up the Instant Pot inner pot. Add the olive oil. When the pot display reads "Hot," add the roast and let sit undisturbed for 6 to 8 minutes to brown the bottom. When the bottom of the roast is browned, turn it over to brown the other side for approximately another 5 minutes.

2. Press Cancel to turn off the sauté function. Spread the butter on top of the roast. Sprinkle with the dry au jus mix and the dry ranch dressing mix. Add the pepperoncinis and ¾ cup (180 ml) water. Secure the lid, ensuring the valve is turned to the Sealing position. Press the Meat/Stew button, and set the time to 45 minutes.

3. Once cooking is complete, allow the appliance to natural release for 20 minutes. After 20 minutes, turn the valve to the Venting position to release the pressure. Press Cancel to turn off the Instant Pot. Carefully remove the lid and transfer the meat and pepperoncinis to a serving platter. Using a fork, shred the beef into large pieces.

4. Press the Sauté button to heat the remaining liquid in the inner pot. As the liquid heats, combine the cornstarch and 1 tablespoon water in a small bowl. When the liquid starts to boil, add the cornstarch mixture, whisking constantly until the sauce thickens. Pour the sauce over the meat. Garnish with chopped parsley. Add additional pepperoncinis to the platter, if desired, and serve.

Mongolian Beef

Yield: 4 Servings | Hands-on Time: 15 Minutes | Cooking Time: 5 Minutes | Total Time: 30 Minutes | Buttons to Use: Sauté and Pressure Cook | Release Type: Natural Release

Who needs fast food and takeout when this meal can be on your table in 30 minutes? This Asian-inspired dish can be served with rice to catch all the garlic- and ginger-laced sauce. For some green, serve with Steamed Broccoli (page 129).

6 tablespoons cornstarch, divided

1 to 1½ pounds (450 to 675 g) flank steak, thinly sliced against the grain

2 tablespoons butter

2 cloves garlic, minced

1 tablespoon fresh ginger, minced

½ red pepper flakes

¾ cup (180 ml) soy sauce

green onions, sliced for garnish

1. Put 4 tablespoons cornstarch in a gallon-sized (3.8 L) zip-top bag. Add flank steak slices and shake well to coat steak evenly.

2. Select the sauté function to heat the Instant Pot inner pot. Press the Sauté button until the panel indicates "More." When the pot reads "Hot," add the butter. When the butter is melted, add the steak strips in one layer. Do not crowd the pot. You may need to brown the beef in two batches. Let the steak sit undisturbed for 3 to 4 minutes, or until it begins to brown. Using tongs, flip the meat over to brown the other side. Repeat with the second batch, if necessary.

3. Add the garlic, ginger, and red pepper flakes and stir well to combine. Press Cancel to turn off the sauté function.

4. Add the soy sauce and ¼ cup (60 ml) water. Stir to combine, using a wooden spoon to scrape up any brown bits from the bottom of the inner pot.

5. Secure the lid, ensuring the valve is turned to the Sealing position. Press the Pressure Cook button and set the time to 5 minutes.

6. Once cooking is complete, allow the pot to natural release for 10 minutes. After 10 minutes, turn the valve to the Venting position to release the pressure. When all the pressure is released, carefully remove the lid. Press Cancel to turn off the appliance.

7. Select the sauté function to complete the sauce. As the liquid heats, combine 2 tablespoons cornstarch with 2 tablespoons water in a small bowl. When the liquid in the pot starts to boil, add the cornstarch mixture and stir continuously until the sauce thickens.

8. Serve over cooked rice. Garnish with green onions.

Beefy Creamy Potatoes Qu Gratin

Yield: 4 Servings | Hands-on Time: 15 Minutes | Cooking Time: 6 Minutes | Total Time: 30 Minutes |
Buttons to Use: Sauté and Pressure Cook | Release Type: Natural Release

If you prefer crispy potatoes, scoop this beefy potato mixture out of the Instant Pot after cooking and place it into a 9 × 11-inch (23 × 28 cm) baking dish. Place the dish under the broiler for 5 to 10 minutes and serve.

1 tablespoon olive oil

½ medium onion, sliced

1 pound (450 g) lean ground beef

2 teaspoons dried Italian seasoning

½ teaspoon salt

¼ teaspoon pepper

2 medium russet potatoes, peeled and sliced ¼-inch thick

2 cups (225 g) shredded sharp Cheddar cheese, divided

¾ cup (180 ml) chicken broth

¼ cup (60 ml) heavy cream

1. Turn on the sauté function to heat the Instant Pot inner pot. When the display reads "Hot," coat the bottom of the pot with olive oil.

2. Add the onions and sauté until translucent, about 3 to 4 minutes.

3. Add the ground beef to the pot and season with the Italian seasoning, salt, and pepper. Sauté for 5 to 7 minutes, until no longer pink, breaking up the beef with a wooden spoon.

4. When the beef is browned, press Cancel to turn off the sauté function. Remove the cooked beef and onion mixture from the pot, leaving the fat at the bottom of the pot. Spray the bottom of the inner pot with cooking spray.

5. Lay a third of the potatoes on the bottom of the inner pot. Top with half of the beef mixture and a third of the cheese. Repeat the layers. Finish with a final layer of potatoes and cheese, reaching the max-fill line, about two-thirds of the way up the inner pot. Do not exceed this line. If necessary, remove some of the potatoes.

6. In a small bowl, mix together the chicken broth and heavy cream. Pour the mixture into the inner pot.

7. Secure the lid, ensuring the valve is set to the Sealing position. Press the Pressure Cook button and set the time to 6 minutes.

8. Once cooking is complete, allow the appliance to natural release for 5 minutes. After 5 minutes, turn the valve to the Venting position to release the pressure. When all the pressure is released, carefully remove the lid. Scoop out to serve.

Ground Beef Stroganoff

Yield: 4 Servings | Hands-on Time: 15 Minutes | Cooking Time: 6 Minutes | Total Time: 25 Minutes | Buttons to Use: Sauté and Pressure Cook | Release Type: Quick Release

Originally a Russian dish from the 1800s, beef stroganoff gained popularity in the United States during the 1950s. This quick, easy, and economical rendition is great for weeknight meals.

3 tablespoons butter

½ medium onion, diced

2 cloves garlic, minced

1 pound (450 g) lean ground beef

8 ounces (225 g) sliced mushrooms

½ teaspoon salt

¼ teaspoon pepper

¼ teaspoon paprika (can used smoked)

8 ounces (225 g) extra wide egg noodles

3 cups (710 ml) beef broth

1 cup (240 g) sour cream, room temperature

chopped Italian parsley for garnish

1. Select the sauté function to heat the Instant Pot inner pot. When the display reads "Hot," add the butter. When the butter is melted, add the onion, and sauté, stirring occasionally until soft, about 2 to 3 minutes.

2. Add the garlic and stir for 1 minute. Add the beef, breaking up into pieces. Cook, stirring occasionally until the beef is no longer pink, approximately 5 minutes. Add the sliced mushrooms, salt, pepper, and paprika, and cook until the mushrooms start to soften.

3. Press Cancel to turn off the sauté function. Add the noodles and beef broth to the inner pot. Stir to combine.

4. Secure the lid, ensuring the valve is turned to the Sealing position. Press the Pressure Cook button and set the time to 6 minutes.

5. Once cooking is complete, turn the valve to the Venting position to release the pressure. When all the pressure is released, carefully remove the lid and stir. Add the sour cream and stir until well combined. Garnish with chopped Italian parsley.

Fresh Salmon with Lemon & Dill

Yield: 2 Servings | Hands-on Time: 5 Minutes | Cooking Time: 3 Minutes | Total Time: 10 Minutes |
Buttons to Use: Pressure Cook | Release Type: Quick Release

A classic flavor profile for salmon, preparing fish can be tricky in the Instant Pot. Make sure to remove fish as soon as possible to avoid overcooking.

2 teaspoons olive oil

2 (6-ounce) (170 g) salmon fillets, skin on

salt and ground black pepper to taste

2 sprigs fresh dill

1 lemon, sliced and seeds removed

1. Place the steam rack inside the Instant Pot inner pot. Add ¾ cup (180 ml) water.

2. Drizzle 1 teaspoon olive oil on each salmon fillet. Season to taste with salt and pepper. Lay one sprig of fresh dill on the flesh side of each fillet. Top with a few slices of lemon.

3. Place the prepared salmon fillets side by side (skin side down) on top of the steam rack inside the Instant Pot inner pot.

4. Secure the lid, ensuring the valve is turned to the Sealing position. Press the Pressure Cook button and set the time to 3 minutes. Once cooking is complete, turn the valve to the Venting position to release the pressure.

5. After all the pressure is released, carefully remove the lid. Remove the salmon fillets using a flexible silicone spatula. Serve immediately.

Tangy Sloppy Joes

Yield: 4 Servings | Hands-on Time: 15 Minutes | Cooking Time: 5 Minutes | Total Time: 25 Minutes | Buttons to Use: Sauté and Pressure Cook | Release Type: Quick Release

Thick, tangy, meaty sloppy joes feature an original homemade sauce that elevates this crowd favorite and weeknight staple. Serve on sandwich buns, over rice, on a baked potato, or any which way you like.

1 tablespoon vegetable oil

1 stalk celery, chopped

½ medium onion, chopped

2 cloves garlic, minced

1 pound (450 g) lean ground beef

1 can crushed tomatoes, 15 ounces (425 g)

½ cup (120 g) ketchup

2 tablespoons tomato paste

2 tablespoons Worcestershire sauce

1 tablespoon vinegar, white or red

several dashes hot pepper sauce, optional

1 tablespoon brown sugar

1 teaspoon dried oregano

1 teaspoon salt

½ teaspoon black pepper

4 hamburger buns, toasted

coleslaw, for serving

1. Select the sauté function to heat the Instant Pot inner pot. When the display reads "Hot," add the oil. Add the celery, onion, garlic, and beef to the inner pot, stirring until the beef is crumbly and no longer pink. Press Cancel to turn off the sauté function.

2. Add ½ cup (120 ml) water and the remaining ingredients except the hamburger buns and stir well. Secure the lid, ensuring the valve is turned to the Sealing position. Press the Pressure Cook button and set the time to 5 minutes.

3. Once cooking is complete, turn the valve to the Venting position to release the pressure. When all the pressure is released, carefully remove the lid and stir well. Press Cancel to turn off the appliance. Select the sauté function. Simmer the sloppy joe meat until the sauce reaches the desired thickness.

4. Serve on toasted buns with a side of coleslaw.

BBQ Baby Back Ribs

Yield: 4 Servings | Hands-on Time: 5 Minutes | Cooking Time: 25 Minutes | Total Time: 40 Minutes |
Buttons to Use: Pressure Cook | Release Type: Natural Release

Setting the ribs under the broiler or on a grill after initially cooking them in the Instant Pot will create that crispy char that defines the flavor of ribs. Don't skip that step!

1 rack (2- to 3- pound) (900 g to 1.35 kg) baby back ribs, cut in half to fit in pot

1 tablespoon salt

1 tablespoon pepper

1 cup (225 g) favorite barbecue sauce, divided

1 cup (240 ml) apple cider (or apple juice)

1. Remove membrane from the back of the ribs, if that has not already been done.

2. Liberally salt and pepper both sides of the ribs. Smear ¼ cup (60 ml) of the barbecue sauce on the meaty side.

3. Pour the apple cider into the Instant Pot inner pot. Lay the ribs into the pot, meaty side down and overlapping if necessary.

4. Secure the lid, ensuring the valve is turned to the Sealing position. Press the Pressure Cook button and set the time to 25 minutes.

5. Turn the oven to broil or heat up the grill shortly before the ribs have finished cooking. Once cooking is complete, allow the appliance to natural release for 10 minutes and then turn the valve to the Venting position to release the pressure.

6. When all the pressure is released, carefully remove the lid. Using tongs, remove the ribs and place them meaty side up on a rack sitting in a rimmed baking sheet. Slather the remaining barbecue sauce on top and place them 4 inches (10 cm) below the broiler for 5 to 10 minutes, or until nicely charred. Remove and serve immediately.

Sweet & Spicy Asian Ribs

Yield: 4 Servings | Hands-on Time: 15 Minutes | Cooking Time: 25 Minutes | Total Time: 45 Minutes |
Buttons to Use: Pressure Cook | Release Type: Natural Release

Sticky, sweet, and a tad spicy, these ribs might be messy to eat, but totally worth it.

FOR THE SAUCE

½ cup (120 g) ketchup

½ cup (100 g) sugar

½ cup (120 ml) soy sauce

3 tablespoons honey

1 tablespoon hoisin sauce

1 tablespoon fresh ginger, minced

2 cloves garlic, minced

½ teaspoon red pepper flakes

FOR THE RIBS

1 rack (2- to 3- pound) (900 g to 1.35 kg) baby
back ribs, cut in half to fit into the pot

1 tablespoon salt

1 tablespoon pepper

½ cup (120 ml) vinegar

1 tablespoon sesame seeds for garnish

2 tablespoons sliced green onions for garnish

To Prepare the Sauce

1. In a small saucepan, combine all the sauce ingredients. Whisk over medium heat until the sugar is dissolved and the sauce begins to thicken.

To Prepare the Ribs

2. Remove the membrane from the back of ribs, if that has not already been done. Liberally salt and pepper both sides of ribs and smear ¼ cup (60 ml) of the sauce on the meaty side.

3. Pour ½ cup (120 ml) water and vinegar into the Instant Pot inner pot. Lay the ribs in the pot, meaty side down, overlapping them as needed.

4. Secure the lid, ensuring the valve is turned to the Sealing position. Press the Pressure Cook button and set the time to 25 minutes.

5. While the ribs cook in the appliance, turn the oven on to broil, or heat up the grill.

6. Once cooking is complete, allow the appliance to natural release for 10 minutes and then turn the valve to the Venting position to release the pressure. When all the pressure is released, carefully remove the lid.

7. Using tongs, remove the ribs and place them, meaty side up, on a rack sitting on a rimmed baking sheet. Slather the remaining sauce on the ribs and place them 4 inches (10 cm) below the broiler for 5 to 10 minutes, or until nicely charred.

8. Remove the ribs from the broiler and top with sesame seeds and green onions. Serve immediately.

> TIP: The ribs can go into the Instant Pot with or without the steam rack. These will work either way.

Hawaiian Shredded Pork

Yield: 4–6 Servings | Hands-on Time: 15 Minutes | Cooking Time: 60 Minutes | Total Time: 90 Minutes |
Buttons to Use: Sauté and Pressure Cook | Release Type: Natural Release

Salty soy sauce, sweet honey, and tangy pineapple combine for a well-balanced barbecue sauce for this island-inspired recipe. Best served as a sandwich or with rice.

FOR THE SAUCE

1 (15-ounce) (425 g) can pineapple chunks with juice, reserved

½ cup (120 ml) reserved pineapple juice

2 tablespoons soy sauce

2 tablespoons honey

3 cloves garlic, peeled and minced

1 tablespoon fresh minced ginger

1 tablespoon chili sauce

½ teaspoon Chinese 5 spice blend

FOR THE PORK

2 tablespoons olive oil

3- to 4-pound (1.35 to 1.8 kg) pork butt (shoulder), cut into 4- to 5-inch (10 to 12 cm) pieces

1 teaspoon salt

½ teaspoon pepper

1 cup (240 ml) reserved pineapple juice

pineapple chunks from drained can

3 green onions, sliced crosswise

Hawaiian rolls and prepared coleslaw for serving

To Prepare the Sauce

1. Open the can of pineapple chunks. Pour out the juice into a small bowl. Set aside the pineapple chunks for later use.

2. In a small saucepan, combine ½ cup (120 ml) of the pineapple juice, soy sauce, honey, garlic, ginger, chili sauce, and Chinese 5 spice blend. Heat over medium-high heat until the sauce thickens. Set aside.

To Prepare the Pork

3. Select the sauté function to heat the Instant Pot inner pot. Add olive oil to coat the bottom of the pot. When the display reads "Hot," add the pork pieces. Let the pork sit untouched for 3 to 4 minutes and then turn the pieces over to sear the other side. Don't overload the pot. This might need to be done in batches.

4. Press Cancel to turn off the sauté function. Add 1 cup (240 ml) of the reserved pineapple juice to deglaze the bottom of the inner pot, using a wooden spoon to scrape up the browned bits.

5. Secure the lid, ensuring the valve is turned to the Sealing position. Press the Pressure Cook button and set the time to 60 minutes.

6. Once cooking is complete, allow the appliance to natural release for 10 minutes; then turn the valve to the Venting position to release the pressure. When all the pressure is released, carefully remove the lid.

7. Using tongs, remove the pork from the pot and place it on a serving platter. Using two forks, shred the pork, removing any large pieces of fat. Season with additional salt and pepper if needed.

8. Pour the Hawaiian sauce over the shredded pork. Top with pineapple chunks and green onions. Serve the meat with Hawaiian rolls and coleslaw.

Beer-Braised Shredded Pork

Yield: 4–6 Servings | Hands-on Time: 15 Minutes | Cooking Time: 60 Minutes | Total Time: 90 Minutes |
Buttons to Use: Sauté and Pressure Cook | Release Type: Natural Release

Beer contributes a pleasant flavor tailor-made for pork dishes. This recipe calls for a dark, malty beer, which will add sweetness to savory beef. Serve up shredded meat on sliders, nachos, tacos (as shown on page J of the color insert), sandwiches, or on top of a salad—the possibilities are endless.

2 tablespoons olive oil

3- to 4-pound (1.35 to 1.8 kg) pork butt (shoulder), cut into 4- to 5-inch (10 to 12 cm) pieces

½ medium onion, sliced

3 cloves garlic, peeled and smashed

1 (12-ounces) (360 ml) bottle dark beer

1 teaspoon salt

½ teaspoon pepper

barbecue sauce of choice, if desired

1. Select the sauté function to heat the Instant Pot inner pot. Coat the bottom of the inner pot with olive oil. When the display reads "Hot," add the pork pieces. Let sit untouched for 3 to 4 minutes and then turn the pieces to sear the other side. Do not overload the inner pot. This might need to be done in batches.

2. When all the pork is browned, add the onion and garlic. Stir well, continuing to sauté another 3 to 4 minutes.

3. Press Cancel to turn off the sauté function. Slowly pour the beer over the pork mixture. Add salt and pepper and stir well.

4. Secure the lid, ensuring the valve is turned to the Sealing position. Press the Pressure Cook button and set the time to 60 minutes.

5. Once cooking is complete, allow the appliance to natural release for 10 minutes; then turn the valve to the Venting position to release the pressure. When all the pressure is released, carefully remove the lid.

6. Using tongs, remove the pork from the inner pot and place it on a platter. Using forks, shred the pork, removing any large pieces of fat. Season to taste with additional salt and pepper.

7. For "crispy edges," spread the shredded pork over a large, rimmed baking sheet. Turn the oven on to broil. When hot, place the meat under the broiler for approximately 5 minutes.

8. Top with the sauce left in the Instant Pot inner pot or with your barbecue sauce before serving.

Pork Loin Roast

Yield: 6 Servings | Hands-on Time: 10 Minutes | Cooking Time: 12 Minutes | Total Time: 30 Minutes |
Buttons to Use: Sauté and Pressure Cook | Release Type: Natural Release

Searing the pork loin roast in butter, garlic, and onions gives this dish great flavor. Turn the juices into a flavorful, creamy gravy to accompany the roast.

---

salt and pepper to taste

2- to 3-pound (900 g to 1.35 kg) pork loin roast

2 tablespoons olive oil

2 tablespoons butter

½ medium onion, sliced

2 cloves garlic, minced

1 teaspoon dried, crushed rosemary

1 cup (240 ml) apple juice

1 tablespoon cornstarch

1. Liberally salt and pepper the outside of the roast.

2. Select the sauté function to heat the Instant Pot inner pot. Coat the bottom with olive oil. When the display reads "Hot," add the butter, onion, garlic, and rosemary. Sauté until the onion softens.

3. Push the onion mixture to the perimeter of the pot and set the roast down into the pot to sear. Leave untouched for 3 to 4 minutes and then turn it over to sear the other side.

4. Press Cancel to turn off the sauté function. Pour the apple juice into the inner pot and secure the lid, ensuring the valve is turned to the Sealing position. Press the Pressure Cook button and set the time to 12 minutes.

5. Once cooking is complete, allow the appliance to natural release for 5 minutes. After 5 minutes, turn the valve to the Venting position to release the pressure. When all the pressure is released, carefully remove the lid and transfer the roast to a serving platter. Tent with foil to rest. Press the Cancel button to turn off the appliance.

6. Press the Sauté button. Combine the cornstarch and 1 tablespoon water. When the liquid starts to boil, whisk in the cornstarch mixture. Continue whisking constantly until the gravy begins to thicken and the desired consistency is reached. Press Cancel to turn off the appliance. Cut into 1-inch-thick (2.5 cm) slices and spoon gravy over the pork loin roast to serve.

Pork Chops Smothered with Onions

Yield: 2 Servings | Hands-on Time: 5 Minutes | Cooking Time: 8 Minutes | Total Time: 20 Minutes |
Buttons to Use: Sauté and Pressure Cook | Release Type: Quick Release

Bone-in chops work the best for this recipes, but boneless can also be used. Just be sure to reduce the cooking time by 3 minutes if using boneless.

2 tablespoons butter

1 medium onion, sliced into 1-inch slices (2.5 cm)

2 cloves garlic, minced

2 (1½-inch thick) (about 4 cm) bone-in pork chops (can use boneless, but reduce cooking time by 3 minutes)

salt and pepper to taste

¾ cup (180 ml) apple cider (or apple juice)

1. Select the sauté function and press the Sauté button again until the heat level switches from "Normal" to "More." When the display reads "Hot," add the butter. Once the butter has melted, add the onion and sauté until it softens. Mix in the garlic and sauté 1 minute more.

2. Push the onion mixture to the perimeter of the inner pot and place the chops into the pot. Season to taste with salt and pepper. Allow pork chops to sit undisturbed for 3 to 5 minutes until the bottom is seared. Once seared, turn them over to sear the other side for another 3 to 5 minutes. If both pork chops do not fit, sear them one at a time. When complete, press Cancel to turn off the sauté function.

3. Remove the chops. Place the steam rack into the inner pot and add the apple cider. Place the chops on top of the steam rack. Secure the lid, ensuring the valve is turned to the Sealing position. Press the Pressure Cook button and set the time to 8 minutes.

4. Once cooking is complete, turn the valve to the Venting position to release the pressure. When all the pressure is released, carefully remove the lid. Remove the chops with tongs and set on a serving platter. Remove the steam rack with tongs. Then use the tongs to remove onions and place them on top of the chops. If desired, serve with cooking liquid.

SOUPS, STEWS & CHILI

ALBONDIGAS SOUP WITH A KICK 86

CLASSIC CHICKEN NOODLE SOUP 88

QUICK & EASY BEEF NOODLE SOUP 90

SPLIT PEA SOUP WITH HAM HOCK 91

CREAMY TOMATO SOUP 92

CREAMY CHICKEN-POTATO SOUP 94

WHOLESOME VEGETABLE RICE SOUP 95

MINESTRONE SOUP 96

CREAMY CHICKEN & WILD RICE SOUP 97

HEALTHY CARROT SOUP 98

SAVORY GROUND BEEF & POTATO SOUP 99

CHICKEN & VEGETABLE SOUP 100

LOADED BAKED POTATO SOUP 102

LASAGNA SOUP 104

KIELBASA & BEAN SOUP 105

BEEF & POTATO STEW 106

GROUND BEEF CHILI 108

GROUND TURKEY & SWEET POTATO CHILI 109

WHITE CHICKEN CHILI 110

Albondigas Soup with a Kick

Yield: 4 Servings | Hands-on Time: 15 Minutes | Cooking Time: 12 Minutes | Total Time: 35 Minutes |
Buttons to Use: Sauté and Pressure Cook | Release Type: Quick Release

Meatballs stuffed with rice and soaked in a tomato-based beefy broth create this satisfying dish—soon to become a go-to favorite.

FOR THE MEATBALLS

1 pound (450 g) lean ground beef

½ cup (90 g) uncooked white rice

¼ cup (15 g) minced parsley

1 fresh jalapeño, seeded and minced

1 egg

1 teaspoon salt

½ teaspoon pepper

½ teaspoon smoked paprika

FOR THE SOUP

1 tablespoon olive oil

1 medium onion, chopped

2 cloves garlic, minced

2 medium carrots, sliced

4 cups (950 ml) beef broth

½ cup (125 g) tomato sauce

1 cup (135 g) frozen peas, thawed

lime wedges for serving

1. Prepare the meatballs in a medium bowl. Combine the ground beef, uncooked rice, parsley, jalapeño, egg, salt, pepper, and paprika. Mix by hand until just blended. Do not overmix. Roll into approximately 15 meatballs, 1½ inch (about 4 cm) diameter each. Place the meatballs on a plate, cover, and set aside.

2. Turn on the sauté function to heat the Instant Pot inner pot. When the display reads "Hot," add the oil and onion. Cook, stirring occasionally, until the onion softens. Add the garlic and cook for an additional minute. Add the carrots, beef broth, and tomato sauce. Mix well.

3. Press Cancel to turn off the sauté function. Add the meatballs to the inner pot one at a time. Secure the lid, ensuring the valve is turned to the Sealing position.

4. Press the Pressure Cook button and set the time to 12 minutes. Once cooking is complete, turn the valve to the Venting position to release the pressure.

5. When all the pressure is released, carefully remove the lid. Add the peas and stir to combine. Serve with lime wedges.

Classic Chicken Noodle Soup

Yield: 4 Servings | Hands-on Time: 10 Minutes | Cooking Time: 5 Minutes | Total Time: 20 Minutes |
Buttons to Use: Sauté and Pressure Cook | Release Type: Quick Release

Never buy canned soup again! Homemade, classic and comforting chicken soup can be on your table in less than 20 minutes! Store a batch in the freezer for easy access when feeling under the weather or for a chilly winter day.

1 tablespoon olive oil

½ medium onion, chopped

3 celery stalks, washed and sliced crosswise

2 medium carrots, sliced

1 pound (450 g) chicken tenders, cut into bite-sized pieces

4 cups (950 ml) chicken broth

½ teaspoon dried rosemary

½ teaspoon dried thyme

¼ teaspoon cayenne pepper

8 ounces (225 g) extra wide egg noodles

salt and pepper to taste

1. Select the sauté function to heat the Instant Pot inner pot. Add the olive oil, onion, celery, and carrots. Stir well and sauté for 2 to 3 minutes.

2. Add the chicken and sauté until all sides of the chicken are lightly browned, approximately 5 minutes. The chicken will not be fully cooked at this point. It will finish cooking during the pressure cook cycle.

3. Press Cancel to turn off the sauté function. Add the broth, rosemary, thyme, cayenne pepper, and noodles. Stir well. Secure the lid, ensuring the valve is turned to the Sealing position. Press the Pressure Cook button and set the time to 5 minutes.

4. Once cooking is complete, turn the valve to the Venting position to release the pressure. When all the pressure is released, carefully remove the lid. Stir well and add the salt and pepper to taste. Serve immediately.

TIP: In the Instant Pot multicooker it is easy to cook a whole chicken and use the cooked chicken in a variety of recipes. This is a great alternative if you prefer shredded chicken in your chicken noodle soup.

To make the shredded chicken, place the steam rack into the Instant Pot inner pot and add 1 cup (240 ml) of water. Season a whole fryer chicken with salt and pepper to taste. Place the whole chicken on top of the steam rack. The Mini will accommodate a 3- to 4-pound (1.35 to 1.8 kg) chicken. Secure the lid, ensuring the valve is turned toward the Sealing position. Press the Pressure Cook button and set the time to 30 minutes. Once cooking is complete, allow the appliance to natural release for 5 minutes. After 5 minutes, turn the valve to the Venting position to release the pressure. When the pressure is released, carefully remove the lid. Using tongs, remove the chicken and place in a bowl. With two forks, shred the chicken meat off the bone.

As an alternative for the Classic Chicken Noodle Soup recipe, skip step 2 and add 2 cups (450 g) of cooked chicken at the end of step 4.

The remaining shredded cooked chicken can be stored for up to 3 to 4 days in the refrigerator and 2 to 6 months in the freezer.

Quick & Easy Beef Noodle Soup

Yield: 4 Servings | Hands-on Time: 10 Minutes | Cooking Time: 5 Minutes | Total Time: 25 Minutes |
Buttons to Use: Sauté and Soup/Broth | Release Type: Quick Release

If you prefer beef to chicken, this noodle soup with similar ingredients is right for you.

1 tablespoon butter

1 pound (450 g) lean ground beef

½ medium onion, chopped

3 stalks celery, sliced

2 medium carrots, sliced

1 dried thyme

½ teaspoon salt

¼ teaspoon pepper

1 can tomato sauce, 8 ounces (225 ml)

8 ounces (225 g) uncooked rotini noodles

4 cups (950 ml) beef broth

1. Select the sauté function to heat the Instant Pot inner pot. When the display reads "Hot," add the butter to the inner pot. When melted, add the ground beef. Cook the ground beef, stirring occasionally, until crumbled and no longer pink, approximately 5 minutes. Add the onion, celery, carrots, thyme, salt, and pepper. Stir and cook until the vegetables soften, approximately 3 minutes.

2. Add the tomato sauce and stir until well combined. Press Cancel to turn off the sauté function.

3. Add the noodles and the broth. Stir just until the noodles are submerged in the broth. Secure the lid, ensuring the valve is turned to the Sealing position. Press the Soup/Broth button and set the time to 5 minutes.

4. Once cooking is complete, turn the valve to the Venting position to release the pressure. When all the pressure is released, carefully remove the lid, stir the soup, and serve.

Split Pea Soup with Ham Hock

Yield: 4 Servings | Hands-on Time: 5 Minutes | Cooking Time: 15 Minutes | Total Time: 30 Minutes |
Buttons to Use: Bean/Chili | Release Type: Natural Release

A smoked ham hock does not have much meat but adds depth and saltiness to a filling soup like this one.

1 pound (450 g) dried split peas

1 leek, washed and sliced, white parts only

1 stalk celery, sliced

1 medium carrot, sliced

1 ham hock, well rinsed

½ teaspoon salt

¼ teaspoon pepper

croutons for serving

1. Add 4 cups (950 ml) water and all dry ingredients, except the croutons, to the Instant Pot inner pot; stir well. Secure the lid, ensuring the valve is turned to the Sealing position. Press the Bean/Chili button and set the time to 15 minutes.

2. Once cooking is complete, allow the appliance to natural release for 15 minutes. After 15 minutes, turn the valve to the Venting position to release the pressure.

3. When all the pressure is released, carefully remove the lid. Remove the ham hock and stir well. The soup will thicken as it sits. For thinner soup, add ½ cup (120 ml) water and stir well. Serve in bowls, and top with croutons, if desired.

Creamy Tomato Soup

Yield: 4 Servings | Hands-on Time: 15 Minutes | Cooking Time: 5 Minutes | Total Time: 20 Minutes |
Buttons to Use: Sauté and Pressure Cook | Release Type: Quick Release

This warm and creamy soup will transport you to your childhood, especially if served with gooey, grilled cheese sandwiches!

---

1 (28-ounce) (800 g) can whole tomatoes

2 tablespoons butter

2 shallots, minced

2 tablespoons brown sugar

2 tablespoons tomato paste

¼ cup (30 g) flour

½ teaspoon salt

¼ teaspoon cayenne pepper

2 cups (720 ml) chicken broth

½ cup (120 ml) cream

2 tablespoons brandy (optional)

TIP: If you do not have an immersion blender, a traditional stand blender can be used. Transfer half the soup at a time to the blender, and then return all of the blended soup to the Instant Pot for the final step.

1. Drain the tomatoes over a fine-sieve strainer into a medium bowl. Break open the tomatoes and scoop out the seeds and pulp. Squish as much of the juice as possible through the strainer into the bowl. Reserve the juice. Place the seeded tomatoes into a small bowl. Discard the seeds and any remaining pulp from the strainer. You should have the medium bowl with the strained juice and a small bowl with the tomatoes.

2. Select the sauté function to heat the Instant Pot inner pot. Add the butter to the inner pot. When the butter has melted, add the shallots and stir for a minute. Add the seeded tomatoes and brown sugar. Allow the tomatoes to sit undisturbed for 2 to 3 minutes, and then flip the tomatoes with tongs to brown the other side. Press Cancel to turn off the sauté function.

3. Add the tomato paste and flour. Stir until the flour is incorporated.

4. Add the salt, cayenne pepper, chicken broth, and reserved juice from tomatoes. Using a wooden spoon, scrape up the brown bits on the bottom of pot. Stir well.

5. Press Cancel to turn off the sauté function. Secure the lid, ensuring the valve is turned to the Sealing position. Press the Pressure Cook button and set the time to 5 minutes.

6. Once cooking is complete, turn the valve to the Venting position to release the pressure. When all the pressure is released, carefully remove the lid. Stir the soup.

7. Using an immersion blender, blend the soup until smooth.

8. Add the cream and stir to incorporate. Add the brandy, if using. Serve as a main dish or as an accompaniment to grilled cheese sandwiches.

Creamy Chicken-Potato Soup

Yield: 4 Servings | Hands-on Time: 15 Minutes | Cooking Time: 10 Minutes | Total Time: 30 Minutes |
Buttons to Use: Sauté and Pressure Cook | Release Type: Quick Release

Although total time to make this is only 30 minutes, buying pre-chopped vegetables like onions, carrots, celery, and garlic at the grocery store will speed up the process even further.

---

2 tablespoons butter

½ medium onion, diced

2 medium carrots, sliced

2 stalks celery, sliced crosswise

2 cloves garlic, minced

1 pound (450 g) boneless, skinless chicken breast, cut into bite-sized pieces (chicken tenders work well for this recipe)

2 medium red skin potatoes, diced into bite-sized pieces

2 teaspoons dried thyme

1 teaspoon salt

½ teaspoon pepper

3 cups (710 ml) chicken broth

½ cup (120 ml) heavy cream

¼ cup (15 g) chopped fresh Italian parsley for garnish

1. Select the sauté function to heat the Instant Pot inner pot. Add the butter. When the butter is melted, add the onion, carrots, celery, and garlic. Cook until the onion softens. Add the chicken and sauté until it has a light golden color. Add the potatoes, thyme, salt, pepper, and chicken broth. Stir well. Press Cancel to turn off the sauté function.

2. Secure the lid, ensuring the valve is turned to the Sealing position. Press the Pressure Cook button and set the time to 10 minutes.

3. Once cooking is complete, turn the valve to the Venting position to release the pressure. When all the pressure has released, carefully remove the lid. Stirring the soup well, mix in the cream.

4. Divide evenly among bowls and garnish with fresh chopped Italian parsley.

Wholesome Vegetable Rice Soup

Yield: 4 Servings | Hands-on Time: 15 Minutes | Cooking Time: 5 Minutes | Total Time: 30 Minutes |
Buttons to Use: Sauté and Soup/Broth | Release Type: Quick Release

Get your veggies on with this flavorful, nutritious, and satisfying plant-based soup. It can be made with any of your favorite seasonal vegetables.

1 tablespoon vegetable oil

½ medium onion, diced

1 jalapeño, seeded and minced

2 cloves garlic, minced

½ cup (90 g) uncooked long grain white rice

1 medium zucchini, sliced

2 medium carrots, sliced

2 stalks celery, sliced

1 cup (110 g) cauliflower florets

4 cups (950 ml) vegetable broth

1½ teaspoons Italian seasoning

½ teaspoon salt

¼ teaspoon pepper

1. Select the sauté function to heat the Instant Pot inner pot. Add the oil to the inner pot. When the pot is hot, add the onions and jalapeño, and cook until softened. Add the garlic and sauté for 1 minute more. Press Cancel to turn off the sauté function.

2. Add the rice, zucchini, carrots, celery, cauliflower, broth, seasoning, salt, and pepper, and stir well. Secure the lid, ensuring the valve is turned to the Sealing position. Press the Soup/Broth button and set the time to 5 minutes.

3. Once cooking is complete, turn the valve to the Venting position to release the pressure. When all the pressure is released, carefully remove the lid. Stir, divide evenly among bowls, and serve.

Minestrone Soup

Yield: 4 Servings | Hands-on Time: 10 Minutes | Cooking Time: 5 Minutes | Total Time: 20 Minutes |
Buttons to Use: Pressure Cook | Release Type: Quick Release

Classic minestrone soup is made with a bounty of vegetables and snappy pasta bites! Stick with small tubular pasta for proper balance, and make sure to top with fresh Parmesan cheese.

½ medium white onion, chopped

2 cloves garlic, minced

1 carrot, sliced

1 stalk celery, sliced

1 small zucchini, sliced into half circle discs

1 cup (110 g) fresh green beans, cut into 2-inch (5 cm) pieces

1 cup (110 g) small tubular pasta

1 (15-ounce) (425 g) can diced tomatoes, drained

1 cup (250 g) red kidney beans, drained (canned or homemade)

1 teaspoon dried oregano

1 teaspoon dried basil

1 teaspoon salt

½ teaspoon pepper

4 cups (950 ml) vegetable broth

Parmesan cheese for serving

1. Put all the ingredients, except Parmesan cheese, into the Instant Pot inner pot and stir well. Secure the lid, ensuring the valve is turned to the Sealing position. Press the Pressure Cook button and set the time to 5 minutes.

2. Once cooking is complete, turn the valve to the Venting position to release the pressure. When all the pressure is released, carefully remove the lid.

3. Stir, divide evenly among 4 bowls, and serve with fresh Parmesan cheese.

Creamy Chicken & Wild Rice Soup

Yield: 4 Servings | Hands-on Time: 10 Minutes | Cooking Time: 25 Minutes | Total Time: 45 Minutes |
Buttons to Use: Soup/Broth | Release Type: Natural Release

Wild rice is native to North America and boasts higher fiber aiding in digestion and lowering cholesterol. It is also a good source of essential vitamins and minerals. In this soup, it adds nutrients along with a hearty bite.

1 pound (450 g) chicken tenders (or breasts) cut into 1- to 2-inch (3 to 5 cm) pieces

¾ cup (135 g) wild rice blend

4 cups (950 ml) chicken broth

8 ounces (225 g) sliced mushrooms

½ medium onion, diced

1 medium carrot, sliced

2 stalks celery, sliced

2 cloves garlic, minced

1 teaspoon dried thyme

1 teaspoon salt

½ teaspoon pepper

¼ teaspoon cayenne pepper

½ cup (120 ml) cream

1. Put all ingredients except the cream into the Instant Pot inner pot and stir well. Secure the lid, ensuring the valve is turned to the Sealing position. Press the Soup/Broth button and set the time to 25 minutes.

2. Once cooking is complete, allow the appliance to natural release for 10 minutes. After 10 minutes, turn the valve to the Venting position to release the pressure. When all the pressure is released, carefully remove the lid.

3. Add the cream and stir the soup until thickened to desired consistency. Serve immediately.

Healthy Carrot Soup

Yield: 4 Servings | Hands-on Time: 10 Minutes | Cooking Time: 8 Minutes | Total Time: 20 Minutes |
Buttons to Use: Sauté and Pressure Cook | Release Type: Quick Release

The coconut milk adds just the right amount of creaminess to this light and healthy plant-based soup. An immersion blender makes pureeing this soup easy, but a stand blender can be used as well. This soup can be served hot or cold.

1 tablespoon olive oil

½ medium onion, diced

1 clove garlic, minced

8 large carrots, peeled and cut into 4-inch (10 cm) chunks

1 (15-ounce) (445 ml) can coconut milk

2 cups (480 ml) vegetable broth

1 teaspoon salt

½ teaspoon pepper

coconut cream for serving

chopped parsley for serving

toasted bread for serving

1. Select the sauté function to heat the Instant Pot inner pot. When the pot displays "Hot," add the oil, onion, and garlic. Sauté until the onion softens. Press Cancel to turn off the sauté function.

2. Add the carrots, coconut milk, broth, salt, and pepper. Stir well. Secure the lid, ensuring the valve is turned to the Sealing position. Press the Pressure Cook button and set the time to 8 minutes.

3. Once cooking is complete, turn the valve to the Venting position to release the pressure. When all the pressure is released, carefully remove the lid.

4. Stir the soup. Blend with an immersion blender or in batches in a stand blender until smooth. Serve hot or cold with coconut cream, parsley, and toasted bread.

Savory Ground Beef & Potato Soup

Yield: 4 Servings | Hands-on Time: 15 Minutes | Cooking Time: 5 Minutes | Total Time: 25 Minutes |
Buttons to Use: Sauté and Pressure Cook | Release Type: Quick Release

This soup can be thrown together in a pinch with everyday ingredients that most home cooks will have on hand.

1 tablespoon butter

1 pound (450 g) lean ground beef

½ medium onion, chopped

2 cloves garlic, peeled and minced

2 medium carrots, sliced

2 cups (300 g) diced potatoes, white or red

4 cups (950 ml) beef broth

1 bay leaf

1 teaspoon salt

1 teaspoon dried thyme

½ teaspoon celery salt

½ teaspoon pepper

several dashes red pepper sauce

¼ cup (15 g) fresh Italian parsley, chopped

TIP: Two medium carrots equal about 1 cup (125 g).

1. Select the sauté function to heat the Instant Pot inner pot. When the display reads "Hot," add the butter. When the butter melts, add the ground beef, onion, and garlic. Stir until the ground beef is crumbly and no longer pink. Press Cancel to turn off the sauté function.

2. Add 1 cup (240 ml) water and the remaining ingredients except parsley, and stir well. Secure the lid, ensuring the valve is turned to the Sealing position. Press the Pressure Cook button and set the time to 5 minutes.

3. Once cooking is complete, turn the valve to the Venting position to release the pressure. When all the pressure is released, carefully remove the lid.

4. Stir well, remove the bay leaf, add the chopped parsley, and serve.

Chicken & Vegetable Soup

Yield: 4 Servings | Hands-on Time: 15 Minutes | Cooking Time: 8 Minutes | Total Time: 30 Minutes |
Buttons to Use: Sauté and Soup/Broth | Release Type: Quick Release

While not claiming that this will cure a cold, this classic soup is chock-full of nutrient-dense vegetables and will surely make you happy and help you feel better!

1 tablespoon olive oil

½ medium onion diced

1 clove garlic, minced

1 pound (450 g) boneless, skinless chicken breasts, cut into 1- to 2-inch (3 to 5 cm) pieces

3 stalks celery, sliced

2 medium carrots, sliced

2 Yukon Gold potatoes, scrubbed and cut into bite-sized pieces

1 (15-ounce) (450 g) can diced tomatoes, drained

8 ounces (225 g) sliced mushrooms

1 teaspoon salt

½ teaspoon pepper

½ teaspoon dried basil

½ teaspoon dried red pepper flakes

½ teaspoon dried rosemary

½ teaspoon dried thyme

4 cups (950 ml) chicken broth

fresh Italian parsley, chopped, for garnish

bread for serving

1. Select the sauté function to heat the Instant Pot inner pot. When the display reads "Hot," add the olive oil, onion, and garlic. Sauté until the onion softens. Add the chicken and sauté another 3 to 5 minutes. Press Cancel to turn off the sauté function.

2. Add celery, carrots, potatoes, tomatoes, mushrooms, salt, pepper, basil, red pepper flakes, rosemary, thyme, and chicken broth. Stir well, and secure the lid, ensuring the valve is turned to the Sealing position. Press the Soup/Broth button and set the time to 8 minutes.

3. Once cooking is complete, turn the valve to the Venting position to release the pressure. When all the pressure is released, carefully remove the lid.

4. Stir the soup, divide evenly among 4 bowls, garnish with parsley, and serve with crusty bread.

Loaded Baked Potato Soup

Yield: 4 Servings | Hands-on Time: 20 Minutes | Cooking Time: 5 Minutes | Total Time: 30 Minutes |
Buttons to Use: Sauté and Pressure Cook | Release Type: Natural Release

This stick-to-your ribs creamy soup topped with salty bacon bits is comfort in a bowl.

12 ounces (340 g) bacon, sliced crosswise into bite-sized pieces

½ medium onion, diced

3 to 4 medium red or white potatoes, scrubbed and cut into 2-inch (5 cm) pieces

1½ teaspoon salt

½ teaspoon pepper

½ teaspoon crushed red pepper flakes

4 cups (950 ml) chicken broth

½ cup (120 g) sour cream

1 cup (115 g) shredded sharp Cheddar cheese

2 tablespoons fresh chives, sliced

bread for serving

1. Select the sauté function to heat the Instant Pot inner pot. When the display reads "Hot," add the bacon pieces and sauté until crisp, approximately 5 minutes. Press Cancel to turn off the sauté function. Remove the bacon with a slotted spoon and place on a paper towel–lined plate. Set aside.

2. Using a hot pad to lift out the inner pot, drain the bacon grease from the inner pot into a heat proof receptacle for disposal. Add the onion, potatoes, salt, pepper, crushed red pepper flakes, and chicken broth. Stir well. Secure the lid, ensuring the valve is turned to the Sealing position. Press the Pressure Cook button and set the time to 5 minutes.

3. Once cooking is complete, allow the appliance to natural release for 10 minutes. After 10 minutes, turn the valve to the Venting position to release the pressure.

4. When all the pressure is released, carefully remove the lid, add the sour cream, and stir well. Add the cheese one handful at a time, stirring until it is melted and fully incorporated.

5. Divide evenly among 4 bowls, top with the reserved bacon and chives, and serve with bread.

Lasagna Soup

Yield: 4 Servings | Hands-on Time: 10 Minutes | Cooking Time: 4 Minutes | Total Time: 20 Minutes |
Buttons to Use: Sauté and Pressure Cook | Release Type: Quick Release

Don't have time to make a full-fledged lasagna? No problem. This easy soup combines classic Italian flavors and is ready in 20 minutes. Dinner is served!

1 tablespoon olive oil

1 pound (450 g) spicy ground Italian sausage

½ medium onion, chopped

3 cloves garlic, minced

½ teaspoon dried basil

½ teaspoon dried thyme

¼ teaspoon dried oregano

¼ teaspoon dried rosemary

1 can diced tomatoes, drained, 15 ounces (425 g)

1 can tomato sauce, 8 ounces (240 g)

4 cups (950 ml) chicken broth

1 cup (75 g) campanelle or bowtie pasta

fresh Parmesan cheese, shredded for serving

½ cup (120 g) ricotta cheese for serving

1. Select the sauté function to heat the Instant Pot inner pot. When the display reads "Hot," add the oil, sausage, onion, and garlic, stirring until the sausage is crumbly and no longer pink. Press Cancel to turn off the sauté function.

2. Add the basil, thyme, oregano, rosemary, tomatoes, tomato sauce, and chicken broth. Stir well. Add the pasta and stir to ensure all pasta is slightly submerged into the liquid.

3. Secure the lid, ensuring the valve is turned to the Sealing position. Press the Pressure Cook button and set the time to 4 minutes.

4. Once cooking is complete, turn the valve to the Venting position to release the pressure. When all the pressure is released, carefully remove the lid.

5. Stir well and divide evenly among 4 bowls. Garnish with Parmesan cheese and a dollop of ricotta cheese, and serve.

Kielbasa & Bean Soup

Yield: 4–6 Servings | Hands-on Time: 2 Minutes | Cooking Time: 50 Minutes | Total Time: 75 Minutes |
Buttons to Use: Bean/Chili | Release Type: Natural Release

This flavorful sausage and bean soup uses a 15-bean soup packet, including seasoning, available at most grocery stores. Just add a pound of sliced sausage, and you've got a low maintenance meal.

1 bag 15-bean soup blend with flavor packet, 20 ounces (570 g)

6 cups (1,420 ml) chicken broth

1 pound (450 g) fully cooked kielbasa, sliced into bite-sized discs

1. Add the bean soup mix, including the seasoning, and broth to the Instant Pot inner pot. Stir well. Secure the lid, ensuring the valve is turned to the Sealing position. Press the Bean/Chili button and set the time to 50 minutes.

2. Once cooking is complete, allow the appliance to natural release for 15 minutes. After 15 minutes, turn the valve to the Venting position to release the pressure. When all the pressure is released, carefully remove the lid.

3. Add the sliced kielbasa and stir well. When the kielbasa is heated through, serve.

Beef & Potato Stew

Yield: 4 Servings | Hands-on Time: 15 Minutes | Cooking Time: 35 Minutes | Total Time: 60 Minutes |
Buttons to Use: Sauté and Meat/Stew | Release Type: Natural Release

This version of the perennial classic is loaded with meat, potatoes, carrots, onions, and peas—all in a savory beef broth.

2 tablespoons butter

1½ pounds (675 g) stew meat
(chuck roast cut into 2-inch [5 cm] pieces)

1 teaspoon salt

½ teaspoon pepper

½ medium onion, coarsely chopped

2 cloves garlic, minced

¼ cup (30 g) flour

½ cup (120 ml) dry red wine

4 cups (950 g) beef broth

2 cups (225 g) baby carrots

2 medium Yukon Gold potatoes, washed and cut into 2-inch (about 5 cm) pieces

3 tablespoons tomato paste

2 teaspoons dried thyme

1 bay leaf

1 tablespoon Worcestershire sauce

2 teaspoons salt

1 teaspoon pepper

1 cup (135 g) frozen peas, thawed

chopped Italian parsley for garnish

1. Select the sauté function to heat the Instant Pot inner pot. When the display reads "Hot," add the butter. Add the stew meat to the pot in a single layer, taking care to not overload the pot. Sprinkle with salt and pepper. Sear undisturbed for 3 to 4 minutes, then flip the meat over with tongs to sear the other side. Repeat with the second batch if necessary.

2. If cooked in batches, return all the meat to the inner pot. Add the onions and garlic. Stir well and sauté for 3 minutes. Sprinkle with flour and stir well to combine. Add the wine to deglaze the pot. Using a wooden spoon, scrape the bottom of the pot to release all the brown bits.

3. Add broth, carrots, potatoes, tomato paste, thyme, bay leaf, Worcestershire sauce, and remaining salt and pepper. Stir well to combine.

4. Press the Cancel button to turn off the sauté function. Secure the lid, ensuring the valve is turned to the Sealing position. Press the Meat/Stew button and set the time to 35 minutes.

5. Once cooking is complete, allow the appliance to natural release for 15 minutes. After 15 minutes, turn the valve to the Venting position to release the pressure.

6. When all the pressure is released, carefully remove the lid, add the peas, and stir well. Remove the bay leaf. Divide evenly among bowls, garnish with parsley, and serve.

Ground Beef Chili

Yield: 4 Servings | Hands-on Time: 10 Minutes | Cooking Time: 15 Minutes | Total Time: 30 Minutes |
Buttons to Use: Sauté and Bean/Chili | Release Type: Quick Release

Chili is great on game day! This version requires little prep and delivers a whole lot of flavor. Serve topped with shredded cheese and some diced red onions for an added punch.

1 tablespoon olive oil

½ medium onion, diced

1 medium green bell pepper, seeded and diced

2 cloves garlic, minced

1 pound (450 g) lean (93%) ground beef

2 tablespoon chili powder

1 teaspoon salt

½ teaspoon oregano

2 tomato paste

1 (10-ounce) (280 g) can tomatoes and chilies

1 (15-ounce) (425 g) can red kidney beans, drained

1 cup (115 g) shredded Cheddar cheese, for serving

½ cup (120 g) sour cream, for serving

½ small red onion, minced, for serving

1. Select the sauté function to heat the Instant Pot inner pot. When the display reads "Hot," add the olive oil, onion, bell pepper, and garlic. Sauté until the onion softens. Add the ground beef and cook until the beef is crumbly and no longer pink. Press Cancel to turn off the sauté function.

2. Add the chili powder, salt, oregano, tomato paste, tomatoes and chilis, red kidney beans, and ¾ cup (180 ml) water. Stir well.

3. Secure the lid, ensuring the valve is turned to the Sealing position. Press the Bean/Chili button and set the time to 15 minutes.

4. Once cooking is complete, turn the valve to the Venting position to release the pressure. When all the pressure is released, carefully remove the lid. Stir the chili well. Divide evenly among bowls and top with shredded cheese, a dollop of sour cream, and a sprinkle of minced red onion.

Ground Turkey & Sweet Potato Chili

Yield: 4 Servings | Hands-on Time: 15 Minutes | Cooking Time: 5 Minutes | Total Time: 30 Minutes |
Buttons to Use: Sauté and Pressure Cook | Release Type: Quick Release

This healthy take on chili is filling and satisfying. Enjoy it, and don't be shy on seconds.

1 tablespoon olive oil

1 pound (450 g) ground turkey

½ medium onion, chopped

2 tablespoons chili powder

1 teaspoon cumin

1 teaspoon garlic powder

1 teaspoon salt

1 cup (250 g) cooked black beans (canned or homemade)

2 large sweet potatoes, peeled and cut into bite-sized pieces

4 cups (950 ml) chicken broth

chopped fresh cilantro for serving

sour cream for serving

1. Select the sauté function to heat the Instant Pot inner pot. When the display reads "Hot," add the olive oil. When the oil is hot, add the turkey and onion. Sauté until the turkey is crumbled and no longer pink. Press Cancel to turn off the sauté function.

2. Add the chili powder, cumin, garlic powder, salt, beans, potatoes, and broth. Stir well, making sure to scrape any brown bits off the bottom of the inner pot. Secure the lid, ensuring the valve is turned to the Sealing position. Press the Pressure Cook button and set the time to 5 minutes.

3. Once cooking is complete, turn the valve to the Venting position to release the pressure. When all the pressure is released, carefully remove the lid and stir well. Divide evenly among bowls and serve with cilantro and sour cream.

White Chicken Chili

Yield: 4 Servings | Hands-on Time: 15 Minutes | Cooking Time: 8 minutes | Total Time: 30 Minutes |
Buttons to Use: Sauté and Pressure Cook | Release Type: Quick Release

This fall favorite is definitely a winner. Top it off with a few diced tomatoes, sliced jalapeños, and a dollop of sour cream. Don't count on leftovers!

2 tablespoons butter

2 shallots, minced

2 cloves garlic, minced

1 pound (450 g) chicken tenders, cut into bite-sized pieces

2 teaspoons chili powder

2 teaspoons cumin

1 teaspoon coriander

1 teaspoon salt

4 cups (950 ml) chicken broth

2 cups (500 g) cooked cannellini beans, canned or homemade

2 (4-ounce) (115 g) cans diced green chilies

1 (10-ounce) (295 ml) can white corn, drained

1 cup (240 ml) heavy cream

juice from ½ lime

diced tomatoes for serving

sliced jalapeños for serving

sour cream for serving

1. Select the sauté function to heat the Instant Pot inner pot. When the display reads "Hot," add the butter. When the butter melts, add the shallots and garlic and sauté for 3 minutes. Mix in the chicken, chili powder, cumin, coriander, and salt. Cook, stirring constantly for 3 minutes.

2. Slowly add broth, scraping all the brown bits off the bottom of the inner pot. Press Cancel to turn off the sauté function.

3. Secure the lid, ensuring the valve is turned to the Sealing position. Press the Pressure Cook button and set the time to 8 minutes.

4. Once cooking is complete, turn the valve to the Venting position to release the pressure. When all the pressure is released, carefully remove the lid.

5. Stir the chili, and add beans, diced chilies, corn, cream, and lime juice. Stir well. Divide evenly among bowls and serve with diced tomatoes, sliced jalapeños, and sour cream.

TIP: This recipe would also work well with ground chicken or turkey. Add in place of chicken tenders and cook until the meat is crumbly and no longer pink. Proceed with the remaining steps in the recipe.

Blueberry–Almond French Toast Casserole, page 10

A

Vanilla Yogurt, page 22

Spaghetti with Meat Sauce, page 34

Red Beans & Rice with Andouille Sausage, page 46

Homemade Hummus, page 48

Hunter Chicken, page 60

F

Mississippi Pot Roast, page 64

Sweet & Spicy Asian Ribs, page 74

Hawaiian Shredded Pork, page 76

Beer–Braised Shredded Pork, page 78

Albondigas Soup with a Kick, page 86

Healthy Carrot Soup, page 98

Loaded Baked Potato Soup, page 102

Whole Fresh Steamed Artichokes, page 120

Warm Chocolate Lava Cake, page 142

Mini Angel Food Cake with Strawberries & Whipped Cream, page 146

VEGGIES

FRESH CREAMED CORN 114

QUICK FRESH CORN ON THE COB 115

BRUSSELS SPROUTS 116

FRESH STEAMED GREEN BEANS WITH SLICED ALMONDS 117

SAUTÉED MUSHROOMS & ONIONS IN GRAVY 118

WHOLE FRESH STEAMED ARTICHOKES 120

STEAMED BABY POTATOES WITH CREAMY ONION GRAVY 122

PERFECTLY FLUFFY BAKED POTATOES 124

CREAMY MASHED POTATOES 125

SWEET POTATO MASH 126

HEALTHY CAULIFLOWER MASH 127

STEAMED ASPARAGUS SPEARS 128

STEAMED BROCCOLI SPEARS 129

CARROTS WITH BUTTER & BROWN SUGAR 130

FRESH BEETS 131

EASY-PEASY SPAGHETTI SQUASH 132

Fresh Creamed Corn

Yield: 4 Servings | Hands-on Time: 5 Minutes | Cooking Time: 3 Minutes | Total Time: 20 Minutes |
Buttons to Use: Pressure Cook | Release Type: Quick Release

Crisp, fresh corn brings this comfort food classic to new heights. This recipe is great year-round but even better during the summer when corn is in season.

4 ears fresh corn on the cob

4 tablespoons butter, cut into pieces

8 ounces (225 g) cream cheese, room temperature and cut into pieces

2 teaspoons sugar

salt and pepper to taste

¾ cup (180 ml) whole milk

¼ cup (60 ml) cream

TIP: Use a bundt pan to cut kernels from the cob. Place the corn on its end in the middle hole. As you carefully slice kernels from top to bottom, they will collect in the pan. Super easy, safer, and no mess!

1. Cut the kernels off each corn cob by standing each ear on end and carefully slicing from top to bottom.

2. Add the kernels to the Instant Pot inner pot. Add the butter and cream cheese. Add the sugar, salt, pepper, milk, and cream. Mix to combine.

3. Secure the lid, ensuring the valve is turned to the Sealing position. Press the Pressure Cook button and set the time to 4 minutes.

4. Once cooking is complete, turn the valve to the Venting position to release the pressure. When all the pressure is released, carefully remove the lid. Stir until thick and creamy. Add additional salt and pepper to taste.

Quick Fresh Corn on the Cob

Yield: 4 Servings | Hands-on Time: 2 Minutes | Cooking Time: 3 Minutes | Total Time: 7 Minutes | Buttons to Use: Steam | Release Type: Quick Release

Avoid standing over a hot stove during the summertime. The Instant Pot transforms fresh corn quickly. When selecting corn, make sure kernels feel plump and plentiful and tassels are brown and sticky to the touch.

4 ears fresh corn on the cob, husks and silk removed

salt and pepper to taste

butter, if desired

1. Place a Genuine Instant Pot Silicone Steamer Basket or steam rack into the Instant Pot inner pot. Add ¾ cup (180 ml) water.

2. Place the corn cobs in the steamer basket or on top of the steam rack, standing them on end. If the corn cobs are too long to fit, cut each one in half and stack them. Secure the lid, ensuring the valve is turned to the Sealing position. Press the Steam button and set the timer to 3 minutes.

3. Once cooking is complete, immediately turn the valve to the Venting position to release the pressure. When all the pressure has released, carefully remove the lid. Using tongs, transfer the corn to a serving dish. Add salt, pepper, and butter to taste, and serve.

Brussels Sprouts

Yield: 4 Servings | Hands-on Time: 10 Minutes | Cooking Time: 0 Minutes | Total Time: 15 Minutes |
Buttons to Use: Sauté and Pressure Cook | Release Type: Quick Release

Brussels sprouts—the nearly perfect superfood! These bite-sized morsels are sure to become a family favorite. The key is to not overcook them; remove them as soon as the timer goes off and transfer to a serving dish.

1 tablespoon butter

1 tablespoon olive oil

1 pound (450 g) medium-sized Brussels sprouts, trimmed and cut in half lengthwise

¾ cup (180 ml) chicken or vegetable broth

salt and pepper to taste

1. Select the sauté function to heat the Instant Pot inner pot. When display says "Hot," add the butter and olive oil. When the butter has melted, add the Brussels sprouts, placing the sliced sides down, if possible. Cook for one minute and then stir. Pour in the broth and scrape any brown bits off the bottom of the inner pot with a wooden spoon or heat-safe spatula.

2. Press Cancel to turn off the sauté function. Secure the lid, ensuring the valve is turned to the Sealing position. Press the Pressure Cook button and set the time for 0 minutes.

3. As soon as the pressure has built in the pot and the display panel reads 0, immediately turn the valve to the Venting position and release the pressure. When all the pressure is released, carefully remove the lid. Immediately transfer the Brussels sprouts to a serving dish. Add salt and pepper to taste. Serve immediately.

Fresh Steamed Green Beans with Sliced Almonds

Yield: 4 Servings | Hands-on Time: 5 Minutes | Cooking Time: 2 Minutes | Total Time: 7 Minutes | Buttons to Use: Pressure Cook | Release Type: Quick Release

Fresh green beans are packed with iron, vitamin B, and calcium. Top them with a little butter and sliced almonds and you've got an elegant side. You will need a Genuine Instant Pot Silicone Steamer Basket for this recipe.

1 pound (450 g) fresh green beans, ends trimmed

1 tablespoon butter

¼ cup (30 g) sliced almonds

salt and pepper to taste

1. Place the Genuine Instant Pot Silicone Steamer Basket into the Instant Pot inner pot. Add ¾ cup (180 ml) water.

2. Place the green beans in the Genuine Instant Pot Silicone Steamer Basket, secure the lid, and turn the valve to the Sealing position.

3. Press the Pressure Cook button and set the time to 2 minutes.

4. Once cooking is complete, turn the valve to the Venting position to release the pressure. When all the pressure is released, carefully remove the lid. Immediately transfer the green beans to a serving dish.

5. Add a pat of butter, sliced almonds, and salt and pepper to taste. Serve immediately.

Sautéed Mushrooms & Onions in Gravy

Yield: 4 Servings | Hands-on Time: 5 Minutes | Cooking Time: 3 Minutes | Total Time: 20 Minutes |
Buttons to Use: Sauté and Steam | Release Type: Quick Release

This decadent mushroom dish is a hearty side or topping for any beef dish.

2 tablespoons butter

½ medium onion, sliced

2 garlic cloves, minced

1 pound (450 g) whole button mushrooms

½ teaspoon salt

¼ teaspoon pepper

¾ cup (180 ml) beef broth

1 tablespoon cornstarch

1. Select the sauté function to heat the Instant Pot inner pot. When the display reads "Hot," add the butter.

2. Once butter has melted, add the sliced onions and sauté, stirring continuously until the onions are soft, about 5 minutes. Add the garlic and sauté for an additional minute.

3. Add the mushrooms, salt, and pepper, and stir to combine. Cook the mushroom mixture for 5 minutes until the mushrooms begin to release their juices. Press Cancel to turn off the sauté function. Pour the beef broth into the inner pot.

4. Secure the lid, ensuring the valve is turned to the Sealing position. Press the Pressure Cook button and set the time to 3 minutes.

5. Once cooking is complete, turn the valve to the Venting position to release the pressure. When all the pressure is released, carefully remove the lid. Press Cancel to turn off the appliance. Press the Sauté button.

6. In a small bowl, stir together the cornstarch and 1 tablespoon water until combined well. Add the cornstarch mixture to the inner pot, stirring continuously for about 2 minutes until the gravy thickens. Remove the inner pot from the appliance and pour the contents into a serving bowl.

Whole Fresh Steamed Artichokes

Yield: 2 Artichokes | Hands-on Time: 5 Minutes | Cooking Time: 14 Minutes | Total Time: 18 Minutes |
Buttons to Use: Steam | Release Type: Quick Release

Steamed artichokes with lemon-butter dipping sauce can now be on your table in less than 20 minutes! Pay attention to the artichoke size to be sure they will fit in the Instant Pot.

2 medium-sized fresh artichokes

4 tablespoons butter

1 tablespoon lemon juice

TIP: Eat artichoke leaves one at a time by scraping the meaty flesh off with your teeth. When you arrive at the center of the artichoke, use a spoon to scrape out the mealy shreds on top of the artichoke heart. When the heart is scraped clean, cut into pieces, dip in the sauce, and enjoy.

1. Cut the stem off each artichoke. Slice 1 inch (2.5 cm) off the top of the artichokes and trim the thorny tips off each leaf. Rinse thoroughly.

2. Place the steam rack in the bottom of the Instant Pot inner pot and add ¾ cup (180 ml) water.

3. Set the artichokes, bottom side down, on the steam rack. Secure the lid, ensuring that the valve is turned to the Sealing position.

4. Press the Steam button and adjust the time to 14 minutes. While the artichokes are steaming, melt the butter in a small dish in the microwave for 20 seconds. Add the lemon juice.

5. Once cooking is complete, turn the valve to the Venting position to release the pressure.

6. When all the pressure is released, carefully remove the lid. Using tongs, lift out the artichokes. Serve with lemon-butter dipping sauce.

Easy-Peasy Spaghetti Squash

Yield: 2–4 Servings | Hands-on Time: 5 Minutes | Cooking Time: 5 Minutes | Total Time: 15 Minutes | Buttons to Use: Pressure Cook | Release Type: Quick Release

Spaghetti squash is a fun and healthy alternative to pasta. Roasting in the oven can take about an hour, but in the Instant Pot it will be ready in 15 minutes. Shred the flesh of the squash using a fork to get that "noodle-like" appearance.

1 fresh spaghetti, or calabash, squash, 6 inches (15 cm) maximum length

salt and pepper to taste

1. Carefully slice the spaghetti squash lengthwise and, using a spoon, scoop out the seeds.

2. Place the steam rack into the Instant Pot inner pot and add ¾ cup (180 ml) water. Set the spaghetti squash halves on top of the steam rack, standing them on end to fit, if necessary.

3. Secure the lid, ensuring the valve is turned to the Sealing position. Press the Pressure Cook button and set the time to 7 minutes.

4. Once cooking is complete, turn the valve to the Venting position to release the pressure. When all the pressure is released, carefully remove the lid. Using tongs, remove the spaghetti squash halves.

5. Place the spaghetti squash on a plate, flesh side up. With a fork, scrape the flesh from the shell toward the center to create long, thin strands of spaghetti squash. Sprinkle with salt and pepper to taste, and serve.

Steamed Baby Potatoes with Creamy Onion Gravy

Yield: 4 Servings | Hands-on Time: 5 Minutes | Cooking Time: 7 Minutes | Total Time: 15 Minutes |
Buttons to Use: Sauté and Pressure Cook | Release Type: Quick Release

A creamy onion gravy that comes together in just a few minutes transforms these savory potatoes.

1 tablespoon olive oil

½ medium onion, sliced

1½ pounds (680 g) baby yellow or red potatoes, approximately 1 to 2 inches (3 to 5 cm) in diameter, washed

½ tablespoon fresh rosemary (or ½ teaspoon dried)

½ tablespoon fresh thyme (or ½ teaspoon dried)

½ teaspoon kosher salt

1 cup (240 ml) chicken broth (or vegetable broth)

1 tablespoon cornstarch

> TIP: Make sure to use whole, small, baby potatoes that are 1 to 2 inches (3 to 5 cm) in diameter for this recipe to ensure thorough, even cooking.

1. Select the sauté function to heat the Instant Pot inner pot. When the display reads "Hot," add the olive oil and onion. Sauté for 2 minutes until the onion starts to soften.

2. Add the baby potatoes, rosemary, thyme, and salt, and stir to combine. Let stand for a couple of minutes so the potatoes begin to sear. Stir well. Press Cancel to turn off the sauté function.

3. Add the broth. Secure the lid, ensuring the valve is turned to the Sealing position. Press the Pressure Cook button and set the time to 7 minutes.

4. Once cooking is complete, turn the valve to the Venting position to release the pressure. Press the Cancel button.

5. When all the pressure is released, carefully remove the lid. Remove the potatoes using a slotted spoon. Press the Sauté button.

6. In a small bowl whisk together the cornstarch and 1 tablespoon water. Pour the cornstarch mixture into the inner pot and whisk into the liquid. Continue to whisk until the liquid simmers and starts to thicken. When the gravy has come to the desired thickness, add potatoes back to the pot and stir to coat well.

7. Serve potatoes topped with the gravy.

Perfectly Fluffy Baked Potatoes

Yield: 4 Servings | Hands-on Time: 2 Minutes | Cooking Time: 14 Minutes | Total Time: 20 Minutes |
Buttons to Use: Pressure Cook | Release Type: Natural Release

Fluffy, steamy, tender baked potatoes are a staple for the meat-and-potatoes type of person. You'll never disappoint with these!

4 medium russet potatoes, scrubbed and pierced with a fork

salt, pepper, and butter to taste

sour cream for serving

chives for serving

TIP: If you want the skin of your potatoes to be crispy, take the fully cooked potatoes out of the Instant Pot, rub them with vegetable oil, and place on a baking sheet in a 400°F (205°C) oven for 10 to 15 minutes.

1. Place the steamer basket or steam rack into the Instant Pot inner pot. Add ¾ cup (180 ml) water.

2. Place the potatoes on the steamer rack, stacking them on top of each other if necessary. Make sure the potatoes are not touching the water. Secure the lid, ensuring the valve is turned to the Sealing position. Press the Steam button and set the timer to 14 minutes.

3. Once cooking is complete, allow the appliance to natural release for 10 minutes. After 10 minutes, turn the valve to the Venting position to release the pressure. When all the pressure is released, carefully remove the lid.

4. Using tongs, remove the potatoes. Slice open lengthwise and top with salt, pepper, and butter. Serve with sour cream and chives or toppings of your choice.

Creamy Mashed Potatoes

Yield: 4 Servings | Hands-on Time: 10 Minutes | Cooking Time: 7 Minutes | Total Time: 20 Minutes | Buttons to Use: Pressure Cook | Release Type: Natural Release

A classic and favorite side dish, this recipe will transform how you prepare mashed potatoes for holiday and weeknight meals alike.

1½ pounds (680 g) yellow potatoes, such as Yukon Golds, cut into quarters

4 tablespoons butter, cut into small pieces

½ cup (120 ml) cream

1 teaspoon salt

1. Place the potatoes and ¾ cup (180 ml) water in the Instant Pot inner pot. Secure the lid, ensuring the valve is turned to the Sealing position. Press the Pressure Cook button and set the timer for 7 minutes.

2. Once cooking is complete, allow the appliance to natural release for 10 minutes. After 10 minutes, turn the valve to the Venting position to release the pressure.

3. When all the pressure is released, carefully remove the lid. Add the butter, cream, and salt. Smash the potatoes to the desired texture, using a potato masher or a fork and a spoon. Add additional salt as needed.

Sweet Potato Mash

Yield: 4 Servings | Hands-on Time: 5 Minutes | Cooking Time: 8 Minutes | Total Time: 20 Minutes |
Buttons to Use: Pressure Cook | Release Type: Quick Release

This one should not be served only at Thanksgiving. Consider adding this healthy side to your weeknight dinner rotation.

2 large sweet potatoes, peeled and cut into large chunks

¾ cup (180 ml) vegetable broth or water

½ teaspoon salt

½ teaspoon pepper

4 tablespoons butter, sliced into 8 pieces

½ cup (120 ml) heavy cream

1. Place the sweet potatoes, vegetable broth, salt, and pepper in the Instant Pot inner pot. Secure the lid, ensuring the valve is turned to the Sealing position. Press the Pressure Cook button and set the time to 8 minutes.

2. Once cooking is complete, turn the valve to the Venting position to release the pressure. Carefully remove the lid. Add the butter and cream, and mash with a handheld potato masher. Add additional salt to taste, and serve.

Healthy Cauliflower Mash

Yield: 4 Servings | Hands-on Time: 5 Minutes | Cooking Time: 3 Minutes | Total Time: 10 Minutes |
Buttons to Use: Pressure Cook | Release Type: Quick Release

Enjoy this healthy and delicious mashed potato alternative. Use an immersion blender to get a super creamy result.

1 large head of cauliflower, cored and cut into large chunks

salt, pepper, and butter to taste

1. Place the Genuine Instant Pot Silicone Steamer Basket or steam rack into the Instant Pot inner pot. Add ¾ cup (180 ml) water.

2. Place the cauliflower chunks into the steamer basket in the Instant Pot inner pot, Secure the lid, ensuring the valve is turned to the Sealing position. Press the Pressure Cook button and set the time to 3 minutes.

3. Once cooking is complete, turn the valve to the Venting position to release the pressure. When all the pressure is released, carefully remove the lid.

4. Drain the cauliflower into a colander. Remove the steamer basket or steam rack from the Instant Pot inner pot and return the cauliflower back to the inner pot. Using an immersion blender, a handheld masher, or two forks, mash the cauliflower to your preferred consistency. Top with salt, pepper, and butter, and serve.

Steamed Asparagus Spears

Yield: 4 Servings | Hands-on Time: 2 Minutes | Cooking Time: 0 Minutes | Total Time: 5 Minutes |
Buttons to Use: Steam | Release Type: Quick Release

Get your folate and vitamins A and C in just a few minutes. The Genuine Instant Pot Silicone Steamer Basket, which that fits into the Instant Pot inner pot is required for this dish.

1 pound (450 g) fresh asparagus spears, bottom 1-inch (2 to 3 cm) trimmed off

salt and pepper to taste

1. Place the Genuine Instant Pot Silicone Steamer Basket in the Instant Pot inner pot. Add ¾ cup (180 ml) water.

2. Place the trimmed asparagus spears in the steamer basket. Secure the lid, ensuring the valve is turned to the Sealing position. Press the Steam button and set the time to 0 minutes.

3. As soon as the display panel reads 0, immediately turn the valve to the Venting position to release the pressure. When all the pressure is released, carefully remove the lid. Immediately transfer the asparagus to a serving dish. Add salt and pepper to taste, and serve immediately.

Steamed Broccoli Spears

Yield: 4 Servings | Hands-on Time: 2 Minutes | Cooking Time: 1 Minute | Total Time: 5 Minutes | Buttons to Use: Steam | Release Type: Quick Release

Top with a pat of butter, some salt and pepper and you've got a healthy, tasty, and super easy side dish. This dish would make a great side for Mongolian Beef (page 66).

1 large broccoli crown

1 pat butter

salt and pepper to taste

1. Slice the broccoli into spears.

2. Place the steam rack in the Instant Pot inner pot. Add ¾ cup (180 ml) water.

3. Place the broccoli spears on top of the steam rack. (A collapsible steamer basket also works well.)

4. Secure the lid and turn the valve to the Sealing position. Press the Steam button and set the time to 1 minute.

5. Once cooking is complete, turn the valve to the Venting position to release the pressure. When all the pressure is released, carefully remove the lid. Immediately transfer the broccoli to a serving dish.

6. Add a pat of butter, salt and pepper to taste, and serve.

Carrots with Butter & Brown Sugar

Yield: 4 Servings | Hands-on Time: 2 Minutes | Cooking Time: 2 Minutes | Total Time: 7 Minutes |
Buttons to Use: Sauté and Steam | Release Type: Quick Release

Butter and brown sugar-coated fresh carrots are sweet and delicious. Try them alongside the Pork Chops Smothered with Onions (page 82).

4 tablespoons butter

¼ cup (50 g) brown sugar

2 cups (225 g) baby carrots

1. Select the sauté function to heat the Instant Pot inner pot. When the display reads "Hot," add the butter. When the butter is melted, add the brown sugar, stirring until the sugar turns to a thick liquid. Add the carrots and stir to coat well.

2. Press Cancel to turn off the sauté function. Add ½ cup (120 ml) water. Secure the lid, ensuring the valve is turned to the Sealing position. Press the Steam button and set the time to 2 minutes.

3. Once cooking is complete, turn the valve to the Venting position to release the pressure. When all the pressure has released, carefully remove the lid. Remove the carrots with a slotted spoon, and serve.

Fresh Beets

Yield: 4 Servings | Hands-on Time: 5 Minutes | Cooking Time: 15 Minutes | Total Time: 20 Minutes |
Buttons to Use: Pressure Cook | Release Type: Quick Release

Vibrant red beets add a touch of elegance to any salad. These beets are tender, flavorful, and ready in less than 20 minutes.

---

1 bunch beets (3 or 4 medium-sized beets)

salt and pepper to taste

TIP: Beautiful red beets produce a lot of excess color. Use gloves to prevent staining your hands, and promptly wipe down any surfaces that come in contact with beet juice to avoid permanent staining.

1. Cut the leafy green stalks and roots off the beets, being careful not to cut into the beet skin. Do not peel beets.

2. Place the steam rack in the Instant Pot inner pot and add ¾ cup (180 ml) water. Place the beets on top of the steam rack. Secure the lid, ensuring the valve is turned to the Sealing position. Press the Pressure Cook button and set the time to 14 minutes.

3. Once cooking is complete, turn the valve to the Venting position to release the pressure. When all the pressure is released, carefully remove the lid. Using tongs, transfer the beets to a plate.

4. Let the beets cool for 5 to 10 minutes. Once cool, turn on the faucet, and run cool water. Use a paper towel to scrub the skin off the beets under the running water. Serve sliced or cubed in salads or as a side dish.

DESSERTS

MINI NEW YORK CHEESECAKES WITH FRESH FRUIT 134

MINI CHOCOLATE CHEESECAKE 136

DECADENT RICH CHOCOLATE BROWNIES 138

TRADITIONAL RICE PUDDING 140

COCONUT-CRANBERRY RICE PUDDING 141

WARM CHOCOLATE LAVA CAKE 142

CINNAMON-SUGAR MUFFINS 144

MINI ANGEL FOOD CAKE WITH FRESH STRAWBERRIES 146

KEY LIME PIE 148

HOMEMADE VANILLA EXTRACT 150

DULCE DE LECHE 151

CANDIED PECANS 152

Mini New York Cheesecakes with Fresh Fruit

Yield: 4 Servings (2 Cakes) | Hands-on Time: 15 Minutes | Cooking Time: 25 Minutes | Total Time: 50 Minutes |
Buttons to Use: Pressure Cook | Release Type: Natural Release

This classic, rich, dense, tangy dessert is easily made and sure to please. Top it with fresh strawberries or blueberries for a beautiful dessert no one will be able to resist. You need two mini springform pans—4-inch (10 mm) and 15-ounce (450 g) capacity—for this dish.

FOR THE CRUST

cooking spray

1 cup (100 g) graham cracker crumbs

3 tablespoons butter, melted

¼ cup (50 g) brown sugar

FOR THE FILLING

8 ounces (225 g) cream cheese, room temperature

¼ cup (60 g) sour cream

1 teaspoon vanilla

¼ cup (50 g) sugar

1 tablespoon cornstarch

1 egg

blueberries and sliced strawberries for serving

To Prepare the Crust

1. Spray 2 mini springform pans with cooking spray. In a small bowl, combine the graham cracker crumbs, melted butter, and brown sugar. Divide the mixture between the two springform pans. Press the crust down with a flat object (the bottom of a small glass works well), allowing the mixture to come up on the sides approximately ½ inch (1 cm). Place the prepared springform pans in the freezer while preparing the filling.

To Prepare the Filling

2. In a medium bowl, blend together cream cheese, sour cream, and vanilla with a hand mixer on medium-low speed. In a separate small bowl, mix sugar and cornstarch. Add half of the sugar mixture to cream cheese mixture and blend until smooth. Add remaining sugar mixture and blend until smooth. Add egg and blend until smooth.

3. Pour filling into pans, dividing equally between each pan. Tap the pans against the counter to eliminate trapped bubbles.

4. Place the steam rack into the Instant Pot inner pot. Add ¾ cup (180 ml) water. Carefully place one springform pan on top of the steam rack and then stack the second springform pan on top of the first. If pans do not neatly stack, cover the bottom pan with heavy-duty aluminum foil and poke several holes in it to vent. Then stack the second pan on top of the foil. The foil will provide support for the top pan.

5. Secure the lid, ensuring the valve is turned to the Sealing position. Press the Pressure Cook button and set the time to 25 minutes.

6. Once cooking is complete, allow the appliance to natural release for 5 minutes. After 5 minutes, turn the valve to the Venting position to release the pressure. When all the pressure is released, carefully remove the lid and take out the pans. Let the pans cool at room temperature for at least 10 minutes. After 10 minutes, run a small paring knife around the inner edges to release the crust from each pan. Remove the springform edge and place the cheesecakes in the refrigerator to cool for at least 4 hours.

7. Run a knife between the crust and the bottom of the pan to release each cake. Remove the bottom of the pan. Top with fresh strawberries and blueberries for serving.

> TIP: When springform pans are stacked on top of each other inside the Instant Pot, pull the stack closer to the front of the pot so the pans do not interfere with the venting mechanism that is toward the back of the pot lid.

Mini Chocolate Cheesecake

Yield: 4 Servings (2 Cakes) | Hands-on Time: 15 Minutes | Cooking Time: 25 Minutes | Total Time: 50 Minutes |
Buttons to Use: Pressure Cook | Release Type: Natural Release

This cocoa dessert will bring out the chocoholic in everyone. You need two mini springform pans—4-inch (10 mm) and 15-ounce (450 g) capacity—for this dish.

FOR THE CRUST

1 cup (100 g) graham cracker crumbs

3 tablespoons butter, melted

¼ cup (50 g) sugar

FOR THE FILLING

4 tablespoons butter

½ cup (90 g) semisweet chocolate chips

8 ounces (225 g) cream cheese, room temperature

½ cup (120 g) sour cream

1 teaspoon vanilla

¼ cup (50 g) sugar

1 tablespoon cornstarch

1 egg, room temperature and lightly beaten

To Prepare the Crust

1. Spray 2 springform pans with cooking spray. In a small bowl, mix together graham cracker crumbs, melted butter, and brown sugar. Divide the mixture into the two springform pans and press the crust down with a flat surface such as the bottom of a small glass. Allow the mixture to come up on the sides approximately ½ inch (1 cm). Place prepared springform pans in the freezer while preparing the filling.

To Prepare the Filling

2. In a small microwave-safe bowl, combine the butter and chocolate chips. Place in the microwave and heat for 1 minute. Remove from the microwave and stir. If needed, return to the microwave for additional time, in 30-second increments, until melted. Set aside.

3. In a medium bowl, blend together the cream cheese, sour cream, vanilla, and chocolate mixture with a hand mixer on medium-low speed. In a separate small bowl, mix together the sugar and cornstarch. Add half of the sugar mixture to the cream cheese mixture and blend until smooth. Add the remaining sugar mixture and blend until smooth. Add the egg and blend until smooth.

4. Remove the springform pans with crust from the freezer. Pour the filling into the pans, dividing equally between each pan. Tap the pans against the counter to eliminate air bubbles.

5. Place the steam rack into the Instant Pot inner pot. Add ¾ cup (180 ml) water. Carefully place one springform pan on top of the steam rack and then stack the second springform pan on top of the first. If pans do not neatly stack, cover the bottom pan with heavy-duty aluminum foil and poke several holes in it to vent. Then stack the second pan on top of the foil. The foil will provide support for the top pan.

6. Secure the lid, ensuring the valve is turned to the Sealing position. Press the Pressure Cook button and set the time to 25 minutes.

7. Once cooking is complete, allow the appliance to natural release for 5 minutes. After 5 minutes, turn the valve to the Venting position to release the pressure. When all the pressure is released, carefully remove the lid and take out the pans. Let the pans cool at room temperature for at least 10 minutes. After 10 minutes, run a small paring knife around the inner edges to release the crust from the pan. Remove the springform edge and place the cheesecakes in the refrigerator to cool for at least 4 hours.

8. Run a knife between the crust and the bottom of the pan to release the cake. Remove the bottom of the pan. Top with fresh strawberries and blueberries.

Decadent Rich Chocolate Brownies

Yield: 4 Servings | Hands-on Time: 5 Minutes | Cooking Time: 30 Minutes |
Total Time: 40 Minutes | Buttons to Use: Pressure Cook | Release Type: Quick Release

Rich, dense, chewy, and of course, chocolaty, these brownies are great on their own but even better with a scoop of French vanilla ice cream on top. You need two mini springform pans—4-inch (10 mm) and 15-ounce (450 g) capacity—for this dish.

cooking spray

4 tablespoons butter, melted

½ cup (40 g) cocoa powder

½ cup (100 g) sugar

⅓ cup (45 g) flour

pinch of salt

½ teaspoon vanilla

1 egg

1 teaspoon powdered sugar for serving

TIP: This recipe can be doubled easily for more chocolaty goodness. Use 2 mini springform pans and stack them on top of each other in the Instant Pot inner pot on top of the steam rack. Do not change the cooking time.

1. Prepare the springform pan by spraying the inside with cooking spray.

2. In a medium bowl, mix together the butter, cocoa powder, sugar, flour, and salt until well-blended. Add the vanilla and egg, and mix until combined.

3. Pour the batter into the prepared springform pan.

4. Place the steam rack into the Instant Pot inner pot and add ¾ cup (180 ml) water. Place the batter-filled springform pan on top of the steam rack.

5. Secure the lid, ensuring the valve is turned to the Sealing position. Press the Pressure Cook button and set the time for 30 minutes.

6. Once cooking is complete, turn the valve to the Venting position to release the pressure.

7. When all the pressure is released, carefully remove the lid, taking care to hold it level so that the condensed water in the lid does not drop on the brownies. Remove the springform pan. Blot the top of the brownie dry with a paper towel if needed. Cool on a wire rack for at least 10 minutes. Once cool, remove the rim of the springform pan.

8. Before serving, sprinkle the brownie with sifted powdered sugar. Remove the bottom of the springform pan. Cut the brownie into 4 pieces and serve.

Traditional Rice Pudding

Yield: 4 Servings | Hands-on Time: 5 Minutes | Cooking Time: 20 Minutes | Total Time: 30 Minutes |
Buttons to Use: Porridge | Release Type: Natural Release

This sweet rice pudding recipe melds together cinnamon, nutmeg, and brown sugar into a perfectly creamy pudding that's dotted with plump raisins.

1 egg

2 cups (480 ml) whole milk

½ cup (120 ml) heavy cream

½ cup (90 g) uncooked short grain white rice

½ cup (75 g) raisins

¼ cup (50 g) brown sugar

1 teaspoon vanilla

¼ teaspoon ground cinnamon

¼ teaspoon ground nutmeg

pinch of salt

TIP: Prefer thicker pudding? After stirring the pudding in step 6, press Cancel to turn off the Instant Pot. Press the Sauté button and continue to cook for 5 minutes, stirring constantly. Be sure to pay close attention during the sauté mode, as the pudding can easily burn.

1. In a small bowl, whisk the egg. Add the milk and cream. Mix well.

2. Pour the milk mixture into the Instant Pot inner pot. Add all the remaining ingredients and stir well.

3. Secure the lid, ensuring the valve is turned to the Sealing position.

4. Select the porridge function and set the time to 20 minutes.

5. Once cooking is complete, allow the appliance to natural release for 5 minutes. After 5 minutes, turn the valve to the Venting position to release the pressure.

6. When all the pressure is released, carefully remove the lid and stir well for a minute or two. The pudding will thicken upon stirring. Divide into 4 bowls and serve immediately. If you prefer it chilled, place in a covered bowl and refrigerate for 2 to 4 hours.

Coconut-Cranberry Rice Pudding

Yield: 4 Servings | Hands-on Time: 5 Minutes | Cooking Time: 20 Minutes | Total Time: 30 Minutes | Buttons to Use: Porridge | Release Type: Natural Release

Here's a flavorful twist on the classic rice pudding recipe. Coconut and cranberries replace the traditional vanilla and raisins. You can add other favorite toppings if you desire.

1 egg

2 cups (480 ml) whole milk

½ cup (120 ml) heavy cream

½ cup (90 g) uncooked short grain white rice

½ cup (90 g) cranberries

¼ cup (50 g) sugar

1 teaspoon coconut extract

¼ teaspoon ground cinnamon

pinch of salt

4 tableapoons dried, sweetened, shredded coconut for topping (1 tablespoon each)

1. In a small bowl, whisk the egg. Add the milk and cream. Mix well.

2. Pour the milk mixture into the Instant Pot inner pot. Add all the remaining ingredients, except the shredded coconut, and stir well.

3. Secure the lid, ensuring the valve is turned to the Sealing position.

4. Select the porridge function and set the time to 20 minutes.

5. Once cooking is complete, allow the appliance to natural release for 5 minutes. After 5 minutes, turn the valve to the Venting position to release the pressure.

6. When all the pressure is released, carefully remove the lid, and stir well for a minute or two. The pudding will thicken upon stirring. Divide into 4 bowls. Top each with 1 tablespoon of the shredded coconut and serve immediately. If you prefer it chilled, place the pudding in a covered bowl, top with the coconut, and refrigerate for 2 to 4 hours.

Warm Chocolate Lava Cake

Yield: 2 Servings | Hands-on Time: 5 Minutes | Cooking Time: 9 Minutes | Total Time: 20 Minutes |
Buttons to Use: Pressure Cook | Release Type: Quick Release

This ooey-gooey, rich chocolate cake is downright sinful. This recipe requires two 5-ounce (150 ml) ovenproof ramekins.

1 teaspoon room temperature butter

2 teaspoons sugar

4 tablespoons butter

½ cup (90 g) semi-sweet chocolate chips

2 eggs plus 1 egg yolk

2 teaspoons vanilla

½ cup (60 g) powdered sugar

3 tablespoons flour

pinch of salt

pinch of cayenne pepper

sifted powdered sugar for serving

raspberries for serving

1. Smear the inside of each ramekin with a little soft butter. Sprinkle 1 teaspoon sugar into each ramekin. Shake and rotate each ramekin around to ensure the entire surface is coated with sugar. Set aside.

2. In a small microwave-safe bowl, combine the butter and chocolate chips. Place in the microwave and heat for 1 minute. Remove from the microwave and stir. If needed, return to the microwave for additional time, in 30-second increments, until melted. Set aside.

3. In a medium bowl, blend the 2 eggs and 1 egg yolk. Add the vanilla and melted chocolate. Mix well.

4. Add the powdered sugar, flour, salt, and cayenne pepper. Mix well until a thick batter forms.

5. Set the steam rack in the inner pot of the Instant Pot. Add ¾ cup (180 ml) water. Pour the batter evenly into the prepared ramekins and set the ramekins side by side on the steam rack.

6. Secure the lid, ensuring the valve is turned to the Sealing position. Press the Pressure Cook button and set the time to 9 minutes.

7. When cooking is complete, turn the valve to the Venting position to release the pressure. When all the pressure is released, carefully remove the lid and take out the ramekins using oven mitts.

8. Let the ramekins sit for 5 minutes. Run a small knife along the inside of the ramekins to loosen the lava cake. Carefully place a small plate over one of the ramekins. Invert so the lava cake comes out of the ramekin and sits upside down on the plate. Repeat for the other ramekin. Top with sifted powdered sugar and serve warm with raspberries.

Cinnamon-Sugar Muffins

Yield: 10 Muffins | Hands-on Time: 5 Minutes | Cooking Time: 9 Minutes | Total Time: 30 Minutes |
Buttons to Use: Pressure Cook | Release Type: Natural Release

A little bit muffin and a little bit donut, this dense baked good combines the best of both sweets. This recipe requires 10 silicone muffin cups, which can be found online or in kitchen supply stores.

cooking spray

1 cup (120 g) flour

¾ cup (150 g) sugar

1 teaspoon baking powder

1 teaspoon ground cinnamon

pinch nutmeg

pinch salt

1 egg

¾ cup (180 ml) milk

1 tablespoon butter, melted

1 teaspoon vanilla

additional granulated sugar for serving, if desired

1. Spray the inside of the silicone baking cups with cooking spray. Set aside.

2. In a medium bowl, whisk together the flour, sugar, baking powder, cinnamon, nutmeg, and salt. Add the egg, milk, butter, and vanilla. Mix well.

3. Divide the batter evenly into the prepared silicone baking cups. Fill each cup two-thirds full, leaving room for muffins to rise.

4. Place the steam rack into the Instant Pot inner pot and add ¾ cup (180 ml) water. Place five of the filled baking cups side by side on the steam rack. The remaining five cups will be cooked in a second batch. Secure the lid, ensuring the valve is turned to the Sealing position. Press the Pressure Cook button and set the time to 9 minutes.

5. Once cooking is complete, allow the appliance to natural release for 10 minutes. After 10 minutes, turn the valve to the Venting position to release the pressure.

6. When all the pressure is released, carefully remove the lid and muffins. Repeat with the second batch. Sprinkle the top of the muffins with additional sugar, if desired. Cool on a cooling rack.

Mini Angel Food Cake with Fresh Strawberries

Yield: 4 Servings | Hands-on Time: 15 Minutes | Cooking Time: 4 Minutes | Total Time: 25 Minutes |
Buttons to Use: Pressure Cook | Release Type: Quick Release

You can stack two 15-ounce (450 ml) mini springform pans for this recipe, although the cakes will be lighter and fluffier if cooked separately.

½ cup (60 g) cake flour or finely sifted all-purpose flour

¼ cup (30 g) powdered sugar

pinch of salt

6 egg whites

1 teaspoon cream of tartar

¾ cup (150 g) sugar

1 teaspoon vanilla (see Homemade Vanilla Extract on page 150)

sliced fresh strawberries and whipped cream for serving

1. In a small bowl, whisk together the cake flour, powdered sugar, and pinch of salt. Set aside.

2. In a large bowl, whip the egg whites using a handheld mixer on medium speed until foamy. Add the cream of tartar and increase the mixer speed to high. Whip until soft peaks form. Continue to whip while adding the sugar ¼ cup (50 g) at a time until fully incorporated. Add the vanilla and whip until incorporated.

3. Turn off the mixer. Carefully fold the cake flour mixture into the egg white mixture until incorporated. Do not overmix.

4. Pour the batter into two ungreased 15-ounce (450 ml) springform pans, filling to the top. Cover the pans loosely with foil, leaving room for the top to expand.

5. Place the steam rack into the Instant Pot inner pot and add ¾ cup (180 ml) water. Place one springform pan on top of the steam rack. Secure the lid, ensuring the valve is turned to the Sealing position. Press the Pressure Cook button and set the time to 25 minutes.

6. When cooking is complete, turn the valve to the Venting position to release the pressure. When all the pressure is released, carefully remove the lid, holding it level to ensure the condensed water does not fall on the cake. Remove the cake with oven mitts. Turn the cake upside down to cool.

7. Repeat steps 5 and 6 for the second pan.

8. Let the cakes cool for an hour and then loosen the sides by running a knife around the inside of each pan. Release the sides of pan and run the knife under the bottom of each cake to release it from the pan bottom.

9. Serve each cake with strawberries and a dollop of whipped cream, if desired.

Key Lime Pie

Yield: 4 Servings | Hands-on Time: 15 Minutes | Cooking Time: 15 Minutes | Total Time: 45 Minutes | Buttons to Use: Pressure Cook | Release Type: Natural Release

This bright, tart, and tangy filling is paired with a sweet, crumbly graham cracker crust. Bring on summertime any time you want! You will need two mini springform pans—4-inch (10 cm) diameter and 15-ounce (450 ml) capacity—for this recipe.

FOR THE CRUST

cooking spray

1 cup (100 g) graham cracker crumbs

3 tablespoons butter, melted

¼ cup (50 g) brown sugar

FOR THE FILLING

2 egg yolks

1 tablespoon sugar

1 (14-ounce) (415 ml) can sweetened condensed milk

¼ cup (60 g) sour cream

½ cup (120 ml) key lime juice

2 tablespoons lime zest

whipped cream for serving

> TIP: If you can't find key limes, you can use 6 tablespoons lime juice mixed with 2 tablespoons lemon juice.

To Prepare the Crust

1. Spray 2 mini springform pans with cooking spray. In a small bowl, mix together the graham cracker crumbs, melted butter, and brown sugar. Divide the mixture into the two springform pans. Firmly press the crust down with a flat object such as the bottom of a small glass. Allow the mixture to come up on the sides approximately ½ inch (1 cm).

2. Place the prepared springform pans in the freezer while preparing the filling.

To Prepare the Filling

3. In a medium bowl, mix the egg yolks and sugar with an electric hand mixer until the mixture is pale yellow.

4. Add the sweetened condensed milk and sour cream to the bowl and blend until well combined. Add the lime juice and lime zest. Blend another minute until fully incorporated.

5. Remove the prepared springform pans from the freezer. Fill each pan to the top with the filling mixture. There may be some extra filling. Cover each springform pan with foil.

6. Place the steam rack into the Instant Pot inner pot and add ¾ cup (180 ml) water. Place one springform pan on top of the steam rack and then stack the second pan on top of the first. Slide the stacked springform pans toward the front of the Instant Pot so they don't interfere with the venting mechanism at the back of the lid.

7. Secure the lid, ensuring the valve is pointed to the Sealing position. Press the Pressure Cook button and set the time for 15 minutes.

8. When cooking is complete, allow the appliance to natural release for 10 minutes. After 10 minutes, turn the valve to the Venting position to release the pressure. When all the pressure is released, carefully remove the lid. Using oven mitts, remove the springform pans.

9. Set the springform pans on a cooling rack for 10 minutes. After 10 minutes, run a knife around the inside of each pan to release the pie from the pan. Carefully release the springform side.

10. Refrigerate the pies for at least 4 hours. To serve, remove the pies from the bottoms of the springform pans by sliding a knife between the crust and the pan. Top the pies with whipped cream and lime zest.

Homemade Vanilla Extract

Yield: 16 Ounces (480 ml) | Hands-on Time: 5 Minutes | Cooking Time: 60 Minutes | Total Time: 120 Minutes |
Buttons to Use: Pressure Cook | Release Type: Natural Release

Store-bought vanilla extract can be pricey, but with this recipe you can make it from scratch. Grade B vanilla beans can be found online and are less expensive than the grade A typically found in grocery stores. A 16-ounce (480 ml) ovenproof glass canning jar is required for this recipe.

---

4 grade B vanilla beans

2 cups (480 ml) 80-proof vodka of choice

1. Slice the vanilla beans lengthwise; then cut each one in half.

2. Place the vanilla beans in the glass canning jar. Fill the jar up to the thread lines with vodka. Place the lid on the glass canning jar, and tighten until fingertip-tight, or until you start to feel resistance when you tighten.

3. Place the steam rack in the Instant Pot inner pot and add ¾ cup (180 ml) water. Place the glass canning jar on top of the steam rack.

Secure the lid, ensuring the valve is turned to the Sealing position. Press the Pressure Cook button and set the time to 60 minutes.

4. When cooking is complete, allow the appliance to natural release for 1 hour. After 1 hour, turn the valve to the Venting position to release the pressure.

5. When all the pressure is released, remove the lid. Using tongs, carefully remove the glass canning jar, and place it on a heat-resistant mat or hot pad. The jar will still be very hot, so be careful to not shock it by placing it on a cold surface, which may cause it to shatter. Store without removing vanilla beans in a cool, dry place. Use as needed.

Dulce de Leche

Yield: 14 Ounces (415 ml) | Hands-on Time: 2 Minutes | Cooking Time: 30 Minutes | Total Time: 45 Minutes | Buttons to Use: Pressure Cook | Release Type: Quick Release

A sweet, rich caramel topping, spoon dulce de leche onto your favorite ice cream or into coffee for a decadent cup of joe. A 16-ounce (480 ml) ovenproof canning jar is required for this recipe.

---

1 (14-ounce) (415 ml) can sweetened, condensed milk

1. Place the steam rack inside the Instant Pot inner pot. Pour the can of sweetened, condensed milk into the canning jar and lightly screw lid on top of jar. Place on top of the steam rack and fill the inner pot with water until the water comes up to 1 inch (2.5 cm) below the top of the jar.

2. Secure the lid, ensuring the valve is turned to the Sealing position. Press the Pressure Cook button and set the time to 30 minutes.

3. Once cooking is complete, turn the valve to the Venting position to release the pressure. When all the pressure is released, carefully remove the lid. Lift out the jar using oven mitts or tongs.

4. Allow the jar to cool to room temperature. Once cool, remove the lid of the jar. Spoon dulce de leche over your dessert of choice.

Candied Pecans

Yield: 2 Cups (454 g) | Hands-on Time: 5 Minutes | Cooking Time: 10 minutes plus 15 minutes in oven | Total Time: 30 Minutes |
Buttons to Use: Sauté and Pressure Cook | Release Type: Quick Release

Pecan halves coated with sugar, vanilla, and warm spices make a special snack or tasty topping for any ice cream or dessert.

2 cups (240 g) pecan halves

¼ cup (50 g) brown sugar

1 teaspoon vanilla

1 teaspoon cinnamon

¼ teaspoon nutmeg

¼ teaspoon seasoned salt

pinch cayenne pepper

cooking spray

1. Select the sauté function to heat the Instant Pot inner pot. Add the pecans, brown sugar, vanilla, cinnamon, nutmeg, salt, and cayenne. Stir well, and sauté until pecans are well-coated. Press Cancel to turn off the sauté function.

2. Add ½ cup (120 ml) water, and secure the lid, ensuring the valve is turned to the Sealing position. Press the Pressure Cook button and set the time to 10 minutes.

3. While the pecans are cooking, preheat the oven to 400°F (205°C). Spray a rimmed baking sheet with cooking spray.

4. When cooking is complete turn the valve to the Venting position to release the pressure. When all the pressure is released, carefully remove the lid, and pour the contents of the inner pot onto the prepared baking sheet. Spread the pecans out into one layer, and place in the oven for 15 minutes.

5. After 15 minutes, remove the baking sheet from the oven. Let it cool completely before serving.

ABOUT THE AUTHOR

Heather Schlueter, J.D. is an attorney turned CEO turned food blogger and author. She loves cooking for her immediate and extended family, which often includes anywhere from 8 to 20 people, six nights per week.

Heather believes that mealtime is a time for love, laughter, happiness, and bonding. This belief drives her passion for serving home-cooked, fresh, and comforting family meals. Her love of writing and communication is the foundation on which she has built her successful professional career. Her blog, The Spicy Apron, combines her passion for cooking and writing in one place.

Heather has crafted her cooking style and built her blog around the motto: Keep it Simple. Keep it Tasty. Keep it Easy to Clean. She is passionate about sharing her years of cooking knowledge with others to help them make mealtime an easy, fun, and enjoyable experience.

Heather lives in Scottsdale, Arizona, with her husband, their eight children (although several are grown and out of the house), and their golden doodle, Bentley.

Find more from Heather at www.TheSpicy Apron.com and on The Spicy Apron Cooking Show YouTube channel.

ACKNOWLEDGMENTS

This book is a labor of love of many. My amazing sister—everyone should be so fortunate to have what we have together—whose food photography always outshines mine and undoubtedly put me in a position to get this fantastic opportunity. My parents who are my biggest fans. All of our children, nieces, and nephews who put up with my you-WILL-eat-a-healthy-and-balanced-diet attitude with smiles on their faces (mostly). The awesome people at Instant Pot® whose support of this book from day one made it all happen. The team at Sterling Publishing—especially Nicole Fisher who ever so patiently answered every single one of my bazillion questions and whose enthusiasm, excitement, and expertise took this book from good to great. And most of all, my wonderful husband whose unwavering love and support for me and all my crazy ideas keeps us grounded on this amazing, exciting, wonderful journey through life together. I'm the lucky one.

INDEX

Albondigas Soup with a Kick, 86–87

Almonds. *See* Nuts

Altitude, cooking times and, ix–x

Angel food cake, mini, with strawberries, 146–147

Artichokes, steamed, 120

Asian ribs, sweet and spicy, 74–75

Asparagus spears, steamed, 128

Baby back ribs. *See* Pork

Bacon

    Crack Chicken, 55

    Loaded Baked Potato Soup, 102–103

Baked potatoes. *See* Potatoes

Bananas

    Coconut-Banana Steel Cut Oatmeal, 18

    Moist Chocolate Chip Banana Nut Bread, 6–7

BBQ Baby Back Ribs, 73

Bean/Chili button, x

Beans and other legumes, 39–49. *See also* Green beans

    Black Beans with Garlic & Onion, 40

    Black-Eyed Peas, 45

    Ground Beef Chili, 108

Ground Turkey & Sweet Potato Chili, 109

Homemade Hummus, 48–49

Kielbasa & Bean Soup, 105

Lentils with Ham, 44

Minestrone Soup, 96

Pinto Beans, 41

Red Beans & Rice with Andouille Sausage, 46–47

Refried Beans, 42

Split Pea Soup with Ham Hock, 91

White Beans with Tomatillo Salsa, 43

White Chicken Chili, 110–111

Beef, 62–70

    Beef & Potato Stew, 106–107

    ground. *See* Beef, ground

    Mississippi Pot Roast, 64–65

    Mongolian Beef, 66–67

    Shredded BBQ Beef Sandwiches, 62

    Toasted Cheesesteak Sandwiches, 63

Beef, ground

    Albondigas Soup with a Kick, 86–87

    Beefy Creamy Potatoes au Gratin, 68–69

    Beefy Macaroni & Cheese, 37

    Ground Beef Chili, 108

    Ground Beef Stroganoff, 70

Quick & Easy Beef Noodle Soup, 90

Savory Ground Beef & Potato Soup, 99

Spaghetti with Meat Sauce, 34–35

Tangy Sloppy Joes, 72

Beer-Braised Shredded Pork, 78–79

Beets, fresh, 131

Berries

    Blueberry-Almond French Toast Casserole, 10–11

    Blueberry-Cream Steel Cut Oatmeal, 19

    Coconut-Cranberry Rice Pudding, 141

    Mini Angel Food Cake with Fresh Strawberries, 146–147

    Mini New York Cheesecakes with Fresh Fruit, 134–135

    Raspberry Coffee Cake, 14–15

Black beans. *See* Beans and other legumes

Black-Eyed Peas, 45

Blueberries. *See* Berries

Boston brown bread, steamed, 12–13

Breads and such

    Blueberry-Almond Crunch Coffee Cake, 16–17

    Blueberry-Almond French Toast Casserole, 10–11

    Cinnamon-Sugar Muffins, 144–145

(continued)

Breads and such (*cont.*)
  Giant Oatmeal Pancake, 20–21
  Moist Chocolate Chip Banana Nut
    Bread, 6–7
  Raspberry Coffee Cake, 14–15
  Steamed Boston Brown Bread, 12–13
Breakfast, 1–23. *See also* Eggs
  Blueberry-Almond Crunch Coffee
    Cake, 16–17
  Blueberry-Almond French Toast
    Casserole, 10–11
  Blueberry-Cream Steel Cut Oatmeal,
    19
  Classic French Toast Casserole, 8–9
  Coconut-Banana Steel Cut Oatmeal,
    18
  Giant Oatmeal Pancake, 20–21
  Moist Chocolate Chip Banana Nut
    Bread, 6–7
  Raspberry Coffee Cake, 14–15
  Steamed Boston Brown Bread, 12–13
  Vanilla Yogurt, 22–23
Broccoli spears, steamed, 129
Brownies, decadent rich, 138–139
Brussels Sprouts, 116
Buttons and their functions, x–xi

Cancel button, xi
Candied Pecans, 152
Carrots
  Beef & Potato Stew, 106–107
  Carrots with Butter & Brown Sugar, 130
  Healthy Carrot Soup, 98
  other soups with. *See* Soups, stews, and
    chili
Cauliflower
  Healthy Cauliflower Mash, 127
  Wholesome Vegetable Rice Soup, 95

Cheese
  Beefy Creamy Potatoes au Gratin,
    68–69
  Beefy Macaroni & Cheese, 37
  Cheesy Chicken & Rice, 58–59
  Cheesy Chicken Salsa Verde, 54
  Creamy Mac & Cheese, 36
  Crustless Quiche, 5
  Loaded Baked Potato Soup, 102–103
  Mini Chocolate Cheesecake, 136–137
  Mini New York Cheesecakes with Fresh
    Fruit, 134–135
  Toasted Cheesesteak Sandwiches, 63
Chicken. *See* Poultry
Chili
  Ground Beef Chili, 108
  Ground Turkey & Sweet Potato Chili,
    109
  White Chicken Chili, 110–111
Chocolate
  Decadent Rich Chocolate Brownies,
    138–139
  Mini Chocolate Cheesecake, 136–137
  Moist Chocolate Chip Banana Nut
    Bread, 6–7
  Warm Chocolate Lava Cake, 142–143
Cilantro-Lime Rice, 27
Cinnamon-Sugar Muffins, 144–145
Citrus
  Cilantro-Lime Rice, 27
  Fresh Salmon with Lemon & Dill, 71
  Key Lime Pie, 148–149
Classic Chicken Noodle Soup, 88–89
Classic French Toast Casserole, 8–9
Classic White Quinoa, 31
Coconut-Banana Steel Cut Oatmeal, 18
Coconut-Cranberry Rice Pudding, 141
Coffee cake, blueberry-almond crunch,
  16–17

Cooking suggestions, xiv–xv
  cornstarch uses, xiv
  crisping things, xiv
  deciding what to cook in pot, xv
  keeping bottom clean, xiv
  overfill precaution, xiv
  pot-in-pot method, xiv–xv
Cooking time
  adjusting with "+"/"–," xi
  altitude affecting, ix–x
  coming to full pressure and, ix
  of recipes. *See specific recipes*
Corn
  Fresh Creamed Corn, 114
  Quick Fresh Corn on the Cob, 115
Cornstarch uses, xiv
Crack Chicken, 55
Cranberries, in Coconut-Cranberry Rice
  Pudding, 141
Creamed corn, fresh, 114
Cream, in Blueberry-Cream Steel Cut
  Oatmeal, 19
Creamy Chicken & Wild Rice Soup, 97
Creamy Chicken-Potato Soup, 94
Creamy Mac & Cheese, 36
Creamy Mashed Potatoes, 125
Creamy Tomato Soup, 92–93
Crisping things, xiv
Crustless Quiche, 5

Decadent Rich Chocolate Brownies,
  138–139
Delay Start button, xi
Desserts, 133–152
  Candied Pecans, 152
  Cinnamon-Sugar Muffins, 144–145
  Coconut-Cranberry Rice Pudding,
    141

Decadent Rich Chocolate Brownies, 138–139

Dulce de Leche, 151

Homemade Vanilla Extract, 150

Key Lime Pie, 148–149

Mini Angel Food Cake with Fresh Strawberries, 146–147

Mini Chocolate Cheesecake, 136–137

Mini New York Cheesecakes with Fresh Fruit, 134–135

Traditional Rice Pudding, 140

Warm Chocolate Lava Cake, 142–143

Dulce de Leche, 151

Dumplings, chicken and, 52–53

Easy-Peasy Spaghetti Squash, 121

Easy-Peel Hard-Boiled Eggs, 2

Egg button (Duo Plus), x

Eggs

Blueberry-Almond French Toast Casserole, 10–11

Classic French Toast Casserole, 8–9

Crustless Quiche, 5

Easy-Peel Hard-Boiled Eggs, 2

Perfectly Poached Eggs, 4

Soft-Boiled Eggs, 3

Fish, Fresh Salmon with Lemon & Dill, 71

French toast casseroles

Blueberry-Almond French Toast Casserole, 10–11

Classic French Toast Casserole, 8–9

Fresh Creamed Corn, 114

Fresh Salmon with Lemon & Dill, 71

Fruit, fresh, mini New York Cheesecakes with, 134–135. See also specific fruit

Giant Oatmeal Pancake, 20–21

Grains. See Pasta; Quinoa; Rice and wild rice

Green beans

Fresh Steamed Green Beans with Sliced Almonds, 117

Minestrone Soup, 96

Ground beef. See Beef, ground

Ground Turkey & Sweet Potato Chili, 109

Gumbo, 56–57

Ham

Crustless Quiche, 5

Lentils with Ham, 44

Pinto Beans, 41

Split Pea Soup with Ham Hock, 91

Hawaiian Shredded Pork, 76–77

Healthy Carrot Soup, 98

Healthy Cauliflower Mash, 127

Heat/Stew button, x

Herbed Rice Pilaf, 28

Homemade Hummus, 48–49

Homemade Vanilla Extract, 150

Hummus, homemade, 48–49

Hunter Chicken, 60–61

Indicator Panel, about, x

Instant Pot Mini

about: this book, recipes and, viii

altitude affecting cooking times, ix–x

buttons and their functions, x–xi

cleaning, xiv

coming to full pressure, ix

cooking suggestions, xiv–xv

deciding what to cook in, xv

Instant Pot (original) and, viii

lid holder, ix

overfill precaution, xiv

pot-in-pot cooking, xiv–xv

pressure release options, xiii

pressure/steam exposure precaution, x

silicone rings, ix

tips for success, ix–xi

using utensils that come with, ix

Keep Warm button, xi

Key Lime Pie, 148–149

Kielbasa & Bean Soup, 105

Lasagna Soup, 104

Lava cake, warm chocolate, 142–143

Lid holder, ix

Lime. See Citrus

Loaded Baked Potato Soup, 102–103

Macaroni. See Pasta

Meat. See specific meat types

Mexican Rice, 30

Minestrone Soup, 96

Mini Angel Food Cake with Fresh Strawberries, 146–147

Mini Chocolate Cheesecake, 136–137

Mini New York Cheesecakes with Fresh Fruit, 134–135

"-" and "+" buttons, xi

Mississippi Pot Roast, 64–65

Mongolian Beef, 66–67

Muffins, cinnamon-sugar, 144–145

Mushrooms

Chicken & Vegetable Soup, 100–101

Creamy Chicken & Wild Rice Soup, 97

Ground Beef Stroganoff, 70

Hunter Chicken, 60–61

Sautéed Mushrooms & Onions in Gravy, 118–119

Noodles. *See* Pasta

Nuts
Blueberry-Almond Crunch Coffee
Cake, 16–17
Blueberry-Almond French Toast
Casserole, 10–11
Candied Pecans, 152
Fresh Steamed Green Beans with Sliced
Almonds, 117
Moist Chocolate Chip Banana Nut
Bread, 6–7
Nutty Brown Rice, 29

Oats
Blueberry-Cream Steel Cut Oatmeal,
19
Coconut-Banana Steel Cut Oatmeal, 18
Giant Oatmeal Pancake, 20–21
Onions
Black Beans with Garlic & Onion, 40
Crustless Quiche, 5
Pork Chops Smothered with Onions,
82–83
Sautéed Mushrooms & Onions in
Gravy, 118–119
Steamed Baby Potatoes with Creamy
Onion Gravy, 122–123
Orzo. *See* Pasta
Oven, crisping things in, xiv

Pancake, giant oatmeal, 20–21
Pasta
about: orzo, 28
alternative (Easy-Peasy Spaghetti
Squash), 121
Beefy Macaroni & Cheese, 37
Classic Chicken Noodle Soup, 88
Creamy Mac & Cheese, 36
Ground Beef Stroganoff, 70

Herbed Rice Pilaf, 28
Lasagna Soup, 104
Minestrone Soup, 96
Quick & Easy Beef Noodle Soup, 90
Rotini Pasta with Creamy
Sausage-Tomato Sauce, 33
Spaghetti with Meat Sauce, 34–35
Pecans, candied, 152
Perfectly Fluffy Baked Potatoes, 124
Perfectly Poached Eggs, 4
Perfect White Rice, 26
Pie, key lime, 148–149
Pinto beans. *See* Beans and other legumes
"+" and "-" buttons, xi
Pork, 73–83. *See also* Bacon; Ham;
Sausage
BBQ Baby Back Ribs, 73
Beer-Braised Shredded Pork, 78–79
Hawaiian Shredded Pork, 76–77
Pork Chops Smothered with Onions,
82–83
Pork Loin Roast, 80–81
Sweet & Spicy Asian Ribs, 74–75
Porridge button, x
Potatoes
Beef & Potato Stew, 106–107
Beefy Creamy Potatoes au Gratin,
68–69
Chicken & Vegetable Soup, 100–101
Creamy Chicken-Potato Soup, 94
Creamy Mashed Potatoes, 125
Loaded Baked Potato Soup, 102–103
Perfectly Fluffy Baked Potatoes, 124
Savory Ground Beef & Potato Soup, 99
Steamed Baby Potatoes with Creamy
Onion Gravy, 122–123
Pot-in-pot cooking method, xiv–xv
Pot roast, Mississippi, 64–65
Poultry, 52–61

Cheesy Chicken & Rice, 58–59
Cheesy Chicken Salsa Verde, 54
Chicken & Dumplings, 52–53
Chicken & Vegetable Soup, 100–101
Classic Chicken Noodle Soup, 88–89
Crack Chicken, 55
Creamy Chicken & Wild Rice Soup, 97
Creamy Chicken-Potato Soup, 94
Ground Turkey & Sweet Potato Chili,
109
Hunter Chicken, 60–61
Weeknight Gumbo, 56–57
White Chicken Chili, 110–111
Pressure
coming to full, ix
natural release, xiii
protecting cabinets from, x
quick release, xiii
release options, xiii
slow release, xiii
Pressure Cook button, xi
Pressure Level button, xi

Quiche, crustless, 5
Quick & Easy Beef Noodle Soup, 90
Quick Fresh Corn on the Cob, 115
Quinoa
Classic White Quinoa, 31
Colorful Quinoa Salad, 32

Raspberry Coffee Cake, 14–15
Red Beans & Rice with Andouille
Sausage, 46–47
Refried Beans, 42
Releasing pressure, options, xiii
Ribs. *See* Pork
Rice and wild rice
about: Rice button, x
Albondigas Soup with a Kick, 86–87

Cheesy Chicken & Rice, 58–59
Cilantro-Lime Rice, 27
Coconut-Cranberry Rice Pudding, 141
Creamy Chicken & Wild Rice Soup, 97
Herbed Rice Pilaf, 28
Mexican Rice, 30
Nutty Brown Rice, 29
Perfect White Rice, 26
Red Beans & Rice with Andouille
    Sausage, 46–47
Traditional Rice Pudding, 140
Weeknight Gumbo, 56–57
Wholesome Vegetable Rice Soup, 95
Rice button, x
Rotini. *See* Pasta

Salad, colorful quinoa, 32
Salmon, fresh, with lemon and dill, 71
Salsa verde, cheesy chicken with, 54
Sandwiches
    Shredded BBQ Beef Sandwiches, 62
    Tangy Sloppy Joes, 72
    Toasted Cheesesteak Sandwiches, 63
Sausage
    Kielbasa & Bean Soup, 105
    Lasagna Soup, 104
    Red Beans & Rice with Andouille
        Sausage, 46–47
    Rotini Pasta with Creamy
        Sausage-Tomato Sauce, 33
    Weeknight Gumbo, 56–57
Sauté button, x
Sautéed Mushrooms & Onions in Gravy,
    118–119
Savory Ground Beef & Potato Soup, 99
Shredded BBQ Beef Sandwiches, 62
Shredded pork. *See* Pork
Silicone rings, ix
Sloppy Joes, tangy, 72

Slow Cook button, x
Soft-Boiled Eggs, 3
Soup/Broth button, x
Soups, stews, and chili, 85–111
    about: blender for, 92
    Albondigas Soup with a Kick, 86–87
    Beef & Potato Stew, 106–107
    Chicken & Vegetable Soup, 100–101
    Classic Chicken Noodle Soup, 88–89
    Creamy Chicken & Wild Rice Soup, 97
    Creamy Chicken-Potato Soup, 94
    Creamy Tomato Soup, 92–93
    Ground Beef Chili, 108
    Ground Turkey & Sweet Potato Chili,
        109
    Healthy Carrot Soup, 98
    Kielbasa & Bean Soup, 105
    Lasagna Soup, 104
    Loaded Baked Potato Soup, 102–103
    Minestrone Soup, 96
    Quick & Easy Beef Noodle Soup, 90
    Savory Ground Beef & Potato Soup, 99
    Split Pea Soup with Ham Hock, 91
    Weeknight Gumbo, 56–57
    White Chicken Chili, 110–111
    Wholesome Vegetable Rice Soup, 95
Spaghetti. *See* Pasta
Spaghetti squash, easy-peasy, 121
Split Pea Soup with Ham Hock, 91
Springform pans, stacking inside Instant
    Pot, 135
Squash, spaghetti, 121
Start, delay button, xi
Steam button, x
Steamed Boston Brown Bread, 12–13
Steamed vegetables
    Fresh Steamed Green Beans with Sliced
        Almonds, 117
    Steamed Asparagus Spears, 128

Steamed Baby Potatoes with Creamy
    Onion Gravy, 122–123
Steamed Broccoli Spears, 129
Whole Fresh Steamed Artichokes,
    120
Steam, protecting cabinets from, x
Sterilize button (Duo Plus), x
Stews. *See* Soups, stews, and chili
Stroganoff, ground beef, 70
Sweet & Spicy Asian Ribs, 74–75
Sweet potatoes
    Ground Turkey & Sweet Potato Chili,
        109
    Sweet Potato Mash, 126

Tangy Sloppy Joes, 72
Toasted Cheesesteak Sandwiches, 63
Tomatillo salsa, white beans with, 43
Tomatoes
    Creamy Tomato Soup, 92–93
    other soups with. *See* Soups, stews, and
        chili
    pasta with. *See* Pasta
Traditional Rice Pudding, 140
Turkey (ground) and sweet potato chili,
    109

Utensils (Instant Pot Mini), ix

Vanilla
    Homemade Vanilla Extract, 150
    Vanilla Yogurt, 22–23
Vegetables, 113–131. *See also specific vegetables*
    Brussels Sprouts, 116
    Carrots with Butter & Brown Sugar, 130
    Creamy Mashed Potatoes, 125
    Easy-Peasy Spaghetti Squash, 121
    Fresh Beets, 131
    Fresh Creamed Corn, 114

(continued)

Vegetables (*cont.*)

Fresh Steamed Green Beans with Sliced Almonds, 117

Healthy Cauliflower Mash, 127

Perfectly Fluffy Baked Potatoes, 124

Quick Fresh Corn on the Cob, 115

Sautéed Mushrooms & Onions in Gravy, 118–119

soups with. *See* Soups, stews, and chili

Steamed Asparagus Spears, 128

Steamed Baby Potatoes with Creamy Onion Gravy, 122–123

Steamed Broccoli Spears, 129

Sweet Potato Mash, 126

Whole Fresh Steamed Artichokes, 120

Warm Chocolate Lava Cake, 142–143

Warm, keep, button, xi

Weeknight Gumbo, 56–57

White Beans with Tomatillo Salsa, 43

White Chicken Chili, 110–111

Whole Fresh Steamed Artichokes, 120

Wholesome Vegetable Rice Soup, 95

Wild rice, in Creamy Chicken & Wild Rice Soup, 97

Yogurt

about: making, 22–23; thermometer for making, 22; Yogurt button and, xi, 22

Vanilla Yogurt, 22–23

Yogurt button, xi, 22